That Dorky Homemade Look

That Dorky Homemade Look

Quilting Lessons from a Parallel Universe

LISA BOYER

Good Books

Intercourse, PA 17534
800/762-7171
www.goodbks.com

Cover and Illustrations by Cheryl Benner
Design by Dawn J. Ranck

THAT DORKY HOMEMADE LOOK
Copyright © 2002 by Good Books, Intercourse, PA 17534
International Standard Book Number: 1-56148-351-6
Library of Congress Catalog Card Number: 2001060208

Library of Congress Cataloging-in-Publication Data
Boyer, Lisa.
      That dorky homemade look : quilting lessons
from a parallel universe / Lisa Boyer.
          p. cm.
      ISBN: 1-56148-351-6
          1. Quilts -- Humor. 2. Quilting -- Humor.
I. Title.
TT835.B635   2002
746.46'02'07--dc21   2001060208

Table
of Contents

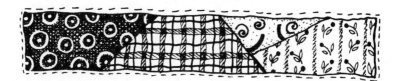

That Dorky Homemade Look

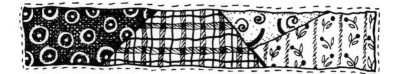

I have a mixed bag of quilting friends. There are some who enjoy quilts as fine art, especially contemporary quilts with their innovative forms and use of color. Some of my friends are strictly traditional. They love the familiar Ohio Stars and Log Cabins and never tire of making them in different colors and settings. Some really love the primitive country look with its plaid backgrounds and charmingly-cut crooked stars. There are many styles to be drawn to, and some beginners dabble in every kind of style before they find their niche.

Personally, it took me 10 whole years of dabbling before I found my quilting identity. Why so long? Because I had to find my own style. As a matter of fact, I had to invent it. I call it the "Dorky Homemade Look."

Now I know what you are thinking. I am not the first person to ever make a Dorky Homemade Quilt. But maybe I will be the first person to define the category as a bona fide art form. I believe this is the first step in public acceptance of the homemade dorky quilt genre, and I have elected myself the spokesperson. As the chief quilt dork, let me outline the steps necessary to make a quilt according to the current Dorky Homemade Quilt guidelines:

1   Pretty fabric is not acceptable. Go right back to the quilt shop and exchange it for something you feel sorry for. Or raid your mother's sewing cupboard. Be careful to avoid the pitfalls of respectable fabrics. Keep your eyes peeled for the suitably tacky. For instance, any fabric left over from the '70s is acceptable in the '90s. Stock up on seafoam green and peach for the new millennium.

2   Realize that patterns and templates are only someone's opinion and should be loosely translated. Personally, I've never thought much of a person who could only make a triangle with three sides.

3   When choosing a color plan for your quilt, keep in mind that the colors will fade after a hundred years or so. This being the case, you will need to start with really bright colors. And don't worry too much about coordinating those colors, because after 200 years, everything turns brown anyway. The only exception to this rule is if you should be lucky enough to find some gaily-colored polyester double-knit. Polyester is forever.

4 Plan on running out of border fabric when you are three-quarters of the way finished. Complete the remaining border with something else you have a lot of, preferably in an unrelated color family.

5 You should plan on cutting off about half your triangle or star points. Any more than that is showing off.

6 If you are doing applique, remember that bigger is dorkier. Flowers should be huge. Animals should possess really big eyes. You just can't go wrong with big-eyed fluffy mammals or rodents used in combination with gigantic hearts and/or mammoth daisies.

7 Throw away your seam ripper and repeat after me: "Oops. Oh well, no one will notice," "Uh-oh, too late now," and "Oh, well, it will quilt out."

8 You should be able to quilt equally well in all directions. I had to really work on this one. It was difficult to make my forward stitching look as bad as my backward stitching, but closing my eyes helped.

9 The most important aspect to remember about Dorky Homemade quiltmaking is that once you have put your last stitch in the binding, you are still only half-finished. The quilt must now undergo a thorough conditioning. Give it to someone you love dearly. They must drag it around the house, wrap themselves up in it when they have a fever, spill something brown on it, and occasionally let Woofie lay on it. It must be washed and dried until it is as soft and lumpy as my Thanksgiving mashed potatoes (for a sample, send 40 cents and a self-addressed, stamped, leak-proof envelope).

Now that I have described the Dorky Homemade Quilt, I'm sure many of you are saying to yourself, "Oh yes, I've seen one of those; it was covering Aunt Wilhelmina's tomatoes during the last frost," or something of the sort.

And I hope you've gained an appreciation for those of us who actually strive to make the quilts that never quite gain "heirloom" status. We deserve recognition for making the kind of quilts that your cat has kittens on, or Grampa Bob covers his tractor with. If we didn't make Dorky Homemade Quilts, all the quilts in the world would end up in the Beautiful Quilt Museum, untouched and intact. Quilts would just be something to *look* at. People would forget that quilts are lovable, touchable, shreddable, squeezable, chewable, huggable objects to wrap themselves up in when the world seems to fall down around them.

Therefore, in the interests of promoting the Dorky Homemade Quilt cause, I urge you to make at least one Dorky Homemade Quilt in honor of all the well-loved quilts that gave their lives for the advancement of our art. Or make one just because it feels good.

Fear
of Florals

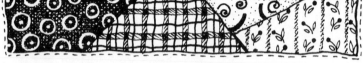

The realization came out of nowhere like a bolt of thunder. There I was, making a block for our guild's Block of the Month. I had just finished piecing together a pretty basket with a bias applique handle, and now I wanted to fill the basket with a nice triangle of floral fabric. I imagined that I would place the floral fabric so that the printed flowers would look like they were jauntily peeking out of the top. There I stood, perusing my colored stacks of fabric in search of a floral that would befit a cheery spring bouquet. After more than a few moments of standing there, eyes narrowed, I was struck by an incredible realization: I did not own a single piece of floral fabric!

Stunned, I sank back into my chair. "How could this be?" I asked myself incredulously. I was in shock. I have been collecting fabric for at least 10 years. I had no idea that I had no floral fabric. Panicking, I tried to think of all the quilts I had ever made. I couldn't remember a single floral fabric in any of them.

I tried to understand what this revelation signified. Did I secretly fear flowers? Did I harbor a distrust of daisies? Was I paranoid about pansies? Would ageratums cause me agitation? Did petunias petrify me?

I'll admit that before I discovered this phlox phobia of mine, I already knew that I had some fears associated with quilting. For example, and don't share this with anyone else, I have always been a little afraid of Sunbonnet Sue. Sure, I know she probably looks innocent to you, but think about it. What is she hiding behind that hat? What if she has a giant, green, convoluted, alien head with red glowing eyeballs and a blood-sucking tentacle mouth? And haven't you noticed that she is hardly ever alone? She's usually appliqued onto a quilt along with her other bonneted alien-head friends, doing something wholesome like pretending to pick flowers or playing patty-cake. And there they are . . . watching you from your bed . . . waiting for you to go to sleep . . . ssleeeeeeep . . .

I also have a fear of quilts with dogs on them. When I see a pieced or appliqued doggie, no matter how cute and cuddly, I can think of only one thing: dog hair. I think I probably acquired this particular phobia back when I was a young bachelorette. The kind of men I usually dated happened to be great big, dog-loving men. (I mean the dogs were great and big, not the men.)

I somehow learned to tolerate their odor (the dogs, that is . . . well, maybe the men, too), but all that dog hair was just too much. Fido's fur covered not only couches and beds and furniture, it found its way into the gourmet bean and weenie casseroles as well.

I often wonder if all that dog hair was some kind of canine territorial-marking strategy. I'll have to admit it was preferable to the other more common form of canine-marking strategy, which was occasionally bestowed upon my handbag. To this day, pictures of dogs on quilts bring back memories of my single years: dog hair in my mouth and a truly unpleasant-smelling purse.

After discovering my apparent floral phobia, I began to wonder if any of my friends were similarly afflicted with quilting fears. Playing amateur psychotherapist at my mini-group, I asked several of my friends what quilting fears they had. Most of them, of course, were afraid to confide in me lest their names end up in some Freudian quilt article like this one. I suppose it was my fault; I sort of got carried away.

I shouldn't have told my friend Selma that her fear of the color pink must be an issue with her femininity. When Binky intimated that she had a fear of polyester, I suggested to her that she had a deep-seated fear of permanence. And when Connie told me that she was afraid of using pastels because they gave her a feeling of "fading away into nothingness," I asked her if she feared her own inevitable demise. I can't understand why they all left so early.

After scaring off all my friends, I decided to call my sister to see if she shared my Fear of Florals. I was somewhat relieved when she told me that she, too, harbored a mistrust of floral fabrics. Her reason was (and I quote), "I'm afraid of using florals because I am afraid of making a quilt that Martha Stewart would describe as 'lovely and pleasing.'" She had a point there. Fear of Martha Stewart. I think I have that one, too.

She also had a few more fears to dispense, such as the Fear of Hand Quilting: "I'm afraid of hand quilting because every book I read about quilting by hand eventually describes how to get blood stains out of fabric. Does this really happen? They advise you to quickly put saliva on the stain. How unsanitary!" Ugh. I never thought about this either . . . Fear of Bodily Fluids on Quilts. Yep, mark me down for that one, too.

By now I was really sorry that I had called her. But alas, she continued: "I'm afraid that in spite of all my planning, pinning, and aligning that my block points won't match. And then some authority-wielding quilt critic will see my quilt and uncover my secret: that I am, in reality, a hopeless, 'pointless' person who is incapable of doing anything well or contributing anything of value. Consequently, my whole existence on this earth would be exposed as 'pointless'!"

Whew. Fear of a Pointless Existence? Gee, compared to that, I guess my Fear of Dog Hair wasn't really so bad after all. I can see now that I should have kept my fears to myself, because now I have acquired a whole new set of things to be afraid of, courtesy of my friends and relatives.

I hope my macabre experience has taught you never to delve into the dark side of the quilting psyche, as there may be things lurking in the inky blackness of your consciousness that will haunt you for the rest of your quilting days—like Sunbonnet Sue, for instance . . .

Oh, Well, No One Will Notice

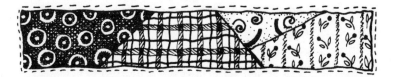

My mother did not have much time in the mornings. After dragging six children out of bed at six a.m., she would haul out the industrial-size Cheerio box, set out the glass milk bottles, and toast entire loaves of bread that she had purchased from the day-old bakery.

I remember her assembly-line lunches: six sets of puffy white bread lined up on top of individual squares of plastic wrap, each set receiving a smear of mayonnaise and/or dollop of mustard, a sprig of crisp romaine lettuce, and a round of cotto salami with peppercorns. An apple and a Scooter pie would then be tossed into each of the little brown lunch bags standing in a row, the name of a child hastily scribbled on each bag. Then she would shoo us out the door into one of three waiting school buses, each of us clutching a different set of homework, sweater, and science project.

It was no wonder then, that upon trying to rush me out the door each morning, a last-minute clothing check might reveal some fashion faux pas, like mismatched socks or a torn dress sleeve. "Oh, well, no one will notice," she would say, as she would pin or pull or tug at the problem unsuccessfully, and then give up and shove me out the door. As a small child, I didn't care if my shoes were on the wrong feet or not and truly believed my mother's theory to be correct. Of course no one would notice.

Then one day in early adolescence (I think it was the same morning that I woke up with breasts), I discovered that my mother's theory, in fact, all of my mother's theories, were hopelessly and dreadfully wrong, wrong, wrong. The world notices everything. Everyone in the whole school would of course notice the big pimple on my chin or the fact that my corduroy pants didn't say "Levi's" on them. How could I face my friends and peers when I was so much less than perfect?

But my mother, upon glancing at my obviously pitiable and un-hip condition, would just wave her hand dismissively and say, "Oh well, no one will notice." Everyone would notice, my life was ruined, and she would never understand, just as surely as the pimple on my chin would never ever go away.

Fortunately, I grew out of this stage (and my chin cleared up, I am happy to report), but after I moved away from home, I began to miss my mother's "Oh, well" attitude toward imperfection. As I had decided in my early adult years that my life would be devoted to the pursuit of perfection, I sometimes missed the balancing, "No one will notice" philosophy of my mother.

My husband was not a suitable substitute. After accidentally sewing a big pucker in a mended garment or perhaps making some curtains for the kitchen that were slightly crooked, I would turn to my husband and ask, "Do you think anyone will notice?"

His face a blank, he would offer, "Notice what?"

"The curtains," I would moan. "The curtains are a half-inch shorter on the right side. Do you think anyone will notice?"

"We have curtains?" he would ask.

"Yes! The kitchen curtains . . . do you think anyone will notice the different lengths?"

"We have a kitchen?"

Obviously, it just wasn't the same.

Now that I am 40 and spend entirely too much time thinking about things like this, I have decided that my mother was a genius. "Oh, well, no one will notice" is an incredibly powerful phrase. When invoked, any problem, large or small, is instantly vaporized and its corresponding worry molecules flung out into the farthest reaches of the universe. I happen to use this phrase abundantly when I am working on a quilt. And it isn't just an excuse for carelessness or laziness either. It's one of my artistic principles.

This fundamental "Oh well, no one will notice" principle of art revealed its profound significance to me a few summers ago. I had mail-ordered a set of six solid, pastel, fat quarters and, upon receiving them, set about making a small Crown of Thorns wall quilt. I had sewn approximately half the quilt blocks when I obtained a new quarter-inch foot for my sewing machine.

I resumed making blocks, not noticing that the new blocks were more than slightly larger than the blocks I had made with my old foot. When I tried placing all the blocks together, the size difference was obvious, but, because I loved that pastel fabric so much, I was determined to set all those blocks together anyway. Pushing and pulling, stretching and easing, I forced all the blocks together. By this time, I had run very low on the pastel fabric and was still short one block, so I made one weird, multi-colored block.

I figured that the quilt was now a lost cause anyway, so I used up the remaining scraps in a half-hearted border attempt. Since the quilt was now pretty lumpy and skewed, I quilted the bejabbers out of it in a heroic effort to make it lay flat.

Sweating profusely, I finally finished the wretched thing. But when my husband tried to hang it on the wall, we noticed that it would not hang straight, because one side was at least one inch shorter than the other. "Oh, well, no one will notice," I sighed, not really believing that anyone with eyesight could help but notice at least one of its multitude of flaws.

That summer, the quilt won Best in Show at the county fair and was published in a major quilt magazine.

Yes, it bothered me that I had been seeking perfection in quilting for so long, and yet my biggest mistake-laden quilt became my proudest achievement. Who can say what happened? Could it be that my mother was right and no one noticed all the mistakes? Or did the mistakes somehow make the quilt better?

I don't really know what the answer is, but since that summer, I learned to look forward to my goofs. I see them now as a creative process. My best quilts have consistently been those in which something happened that I hadn't planned. I make "mistakes" now on purpose because I love their effect, not just the effect I am able to achieve in fabric, but the effect on the public as well. Some people laugh, some people scratch their heads, some people won't forgive, but take my word for it, they *all* notice.

Learning to Sew in a Parallel Universe

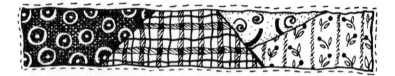

My sister called me last night to discuss another urgent and important quilt matter. (I have a red phone especially designated for this purpose. I got the idea from Batman.) In the course of the conversation, I asked her what memories of sewing she had as a child. She remembered, as I did, that many department stores had a fabric department at that time. Some of the stores even had cafeterias. The department store our mother took us to most often was at the La Mirada Shopping Center. I don't think the word "mall" was invented at the time; they were all "shopping centers."

My sister described the fabric department as a world of wonder, full of limitless possibilities. There was so much fabric just waiting to be made into dresses. There were huge pattern books to sit and peruse. And if that wasn't wonderful enough, the buttons, zippers, braids, rick-rack, binding . . . well, there just wasn't enough time or money in the universe to make everything you wanted.

My mother used to let her pick out her own patterns and fabric. And even though money was tight, the fabric and pattern money were always there. My sister would sit out in the enclosed patio where my mother's sewing machine was located and sew three of the same dress in different fabrics, usually all in one day. She loved sewing. She could hardly keep her joy contained as she recounted all of this to me.

It was then that I realized that I must have been raised in a parallel universe and wasn't returned until I was 29. In my universe, when I was a child, the department store fabric shop wasn't wonderful at all. It smelled like formaldehyde and tuna fish, and there was this mean saleslady there who had black spiders hiding in her hair. When we got there, my mother would sit down for a 12-hour stint in front of the pattern books.

Fighting off a formaldehyde headache, I would play with the button rack, and the mean saleslady would glare at me and mutter her evil incantations. Then I would go over to the fabrics and wrap myself up in the small portions trailing off the bolts, and the mean saleslady would shriek at me not to touch the fabric. Then I would go to the pattern books and leaf through the boring pictures of skinny women in bouffant hairdos, looking like they were expecting company at any minute. I thought they would make great paper dolls, but the mean saleslady told me that if I touched the scissors she would eat me.

Finally, my mother would settle on a pattern, purchase the fabric, and make me some sort of dress. I can't remember any of the dresses, but I sure remember the shoes that went with them. They hurt like the dickens. Sewing held no magic for me; I just wanted to take my shoes off.

When I got to junior high school, I decided to take Home Ec (pronounced Home Eccchhh) and finally learn to sew like my sister. Coincidentally, at this time, my mother won a free sewing machine. It came right in the mail, through a scratch-off postcard. What my mother didn't know at the time was that everyone else in the neighborhood won one also.

The gimmick was that you got a free sewing machine (probably made in some underprivileged country by five-year olds on 12-hour shifts while their mothers looked at pattern books), and all you had to do was come in and claim it. That is, *try* to claim it from a shark of a salesman who wouldn't let a free machine out the door unless it was accompanied by a $400 sewing-machine cabinet.

Well, that salesman was no match for my mother. She went down to that ol' sewing machine store and invoked the name of every consumer advocacy agency she could think of, as well as the Better Business Bureau, Chamber of Commerce, and the President. Needless to say, she left with a free sewing machine in a cardboard case. Weighing only 300 pounds, it was completely portable and perfect for the new seam-stress-to-be in the family, namely, me.

For all of you who own quality sewing machines, it is difficult to even begin to understand the agony of sewing on a cheap machine. Now take your imagination a step further and try to picture what sewing on a "free" sewing machine is like. The beast would whine and wheeze and skip and vomit up great wads of thread every chance it got.

I lugged that monster to school every day of the school year, and, for my efforts, I became the proud owner of my own custom-made gym bag. I also made a dress, but I don't want to talk about it.

Needless to say, I didn't think much of the sewing experience. Then when I was 25, I met my husband, who had a penchant for old cars and loved to restore them himself. He bought me a dependable sewing machine, and, somehow, I got roped into doing the interior upholstery of a 1949 Packard. I just tried to imagine that all the seats were really giant gym bags, more or less. The interior came out beautifully! After that, I curtained, slipcovered, and pillowed every inch of my house with my more-or-less gym bags. Then, one magical day at the age of 29, I took my first quilting class. I have been in love with sewing ever since. At the same time, I also developed a love for fine old sewing machines because of the "free" sewing-machine experience.

So no matter what universe each of us came from, my sister and I arrived at exactly the same place. And each new project we undertake, we undertake from different backgrounds and levels of experience. For my sister, quilting is a relatively recent departure from a rich and varied sewing history, beginning from the time she was a little girl dreaming about the limitless possibilities of fabrics and patterns. For me, everything still looks like a gym bag, but fortunately does not smell like tuna fish.

Color Theory
for Quilters

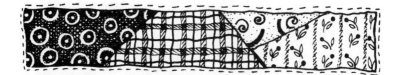

Ha! I got your attention with the title, didn't I? And do you know why I did? Because each one of us, no matter how many beautiful quilts or awards to our credit, has a deep-seated color anxiety. And do you know why this is? Because somewhere along the line, someone made you think that it all made sense, and only *you* didn't quite get it.

I have now come to learn, through contacting various secret governmental agencies and speaking to numerous high-ranking thinktank scientists, that there really is no color theory at all.

There, isn't that liberating? Don't you feel better? Now you can plop together whatever you very well please and be confident that you will not be breaking any known physical laws of the universe.

Too bad I'm lying. But didn't it feel good for just a few moments? I came up with the scenario above as a secret fantasy after taking yet another color theory class for quilters. I guess I keep hoping for some teacher to impart a magical color truth that makes it all so obvious and allows me to gain some control over those dread colors once and for all. But alas, at some key point in every lecture, the speaker pulls out the dreaded color wheel. "Oh no," I cry, "you're not going to drag out one of those things, are you?" And I plunge again into the hopeless, hacking jowls of despair.

I hate the color wheel. I mean, doesn't it just *look* wicked? C'mon, you know what I mean—that hexagonal multi-color star inside that ring of evil? Why, I'll bet in the 17th century, if you had one of those painted on your barn, you would have been burned at the stake. And how about those colors on that thing? Who on earth has any fabrics in their stash that actually look like anything on there?

I once asked a teacher this question. Specifically, I asked where unbleached muslin might fit on that wheel. She grinned and pulled out this weird poster that must have been three feet square, just showing the effect of adding different amounts of black and white to yellow and green. There must have been 4,000 little gradations on that board. At that point, I knew I would never ever get it.

I guess I really should have known it all along. I am not an artist. My background is in science. And being a scientist, I know that color is light, and light travels in waves. I have never been good at waves. My hair doesn't curl and I get sick on boats. Besides, sound also travels in waves, and I was a failure at piano, too. And while we are on the subject of wave science, have you ever seen a physicist whose clothes matched? If they don't get it, I guess I don't have a chance at all.

So let's give up this silly charade once and for all and just admit that colors do whatever suits them. They aren't the least bit intimidated by that color wheel you have hanging on your sewing-room wall. Believe me, I really have tried all this color theory stuff, but so many aspects of it just don't ring true. Take, for instance, complementary colors. Ha! I use them all the time and never get any compliments.

Besides, I have developed my own theory of color. I believe that color is all in our brains anyway, which is very interesting if you think about it. The brain itself happens to be a very ugly color of gray, kind of like already-chewed gum. Think about that gray, gummy, lumpy blob sitting in your skull, perceiving and imagining all those beautiful colors. (Kind of makes you want to skip lunch, doesn't it?) Did *your* gray, gummy blob ever have to consult a color wheel in order to appreciate a rainbow? I rest my case.

The Genetics of Quilting Tools

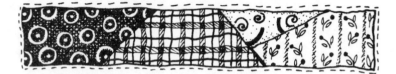

How I love a good sewing tool. The way a fine pair of heavy steel scissors feels snipping and snapping in my hand, a slick new rotary blade slicing through fabric like butter, a pack of strong and fine pins lining up wily seams, a well fitting-thimble—what could be better?

I have a thing for scissors. Now I love rotary cutters too, but there is something so fundamental, so primal, about a good pair of scissors. I have a separate pair of scissors for everything, because as a real scissors connoisseur, I know that snipping, trimming, slicing, nipping, cutting, and slashing are entirely unrelated functions and each requires a highly sophisticated and specialized tool. I can't help it. My scissors passion is a genetic trait that I inherited from my mother. (The scissors gene is located right next to the big ankles gene, and I got them both. My sister got the rotary cutter gene that comes with nice ankles.)

My mother owned one really nice pair of scissors, but she would never let us use them. She kept them hidden away in a forbidden spot; we were never to touch or gaze upon the "good scissors." I remember thinking as a child that my mother having "good" scissors meant that the rest of the scissors in the house must somehow be evil.

When on some rare occasion she would leave them out, I would sneak them away and go cut something. (How could they get me in trouble? They were "good" scissors.) Electrical wires were fun to cut. Raisins used to scream and beg for mercy before I would snip them and all their little raisin friends apart. My problem was that I was never smart enough to replace the scissors (or clean the raisin guts off) before my mother discovered their absence. Shortly after my crime, a shrill cry would come keening out of her bedroom, just like the spooky golden arm story. Only instead of a golden arm, the monster would want to know, "Whhhoooo's got my gooooooood scissorsssssssss????"

So when I grew up (I'll let you know if the process ever completes itself), I treated myself to several pairs of good scissors. But then I thought I would be smarter than my mother was: I bought 15 pairs of crummy decoy scissors and left a pair in every drawer in the house. But alas, my son inherited the big-ankle/scissors-loving chromosome and is not at all fooled by this strategy. And so I have to rise up out of my lair just like my mother did, trailing threads and fabric behind me like some evil swamp monster, to rescue the raisin men from mean Mr. Snippy.

My husband, fortunately, did not inherit a love of good scissors from his mother and cannot fathom why I need so many pairs of scissors. I, on the other hand, cannot understand his fascination with my pins. Yes, they are the really nice, fine, glass-headed, steel-shank kind, but I don't really think the quality matters to him. It's all the miraculous minor surgeries he can perform with them. It's not so much that I mind him playing doctor with my stuff, but what really grosses me out is when he puts them back after he's done. Ugh.

I ask you, is it any wonder then, that when he tries to cross my sewing room floor, that any pin lying innocently on the floor minding its own business would try to defend itself by hurling itself into his foot? (I wonder if magnetic feet are hereditary, too. They're probably on the rusty old tractor chromosome.)

And while we are talking about attracting things, I have to tell you about another tool I love. I adore old mechanical sewing machines, and stray machines follow me home all the time. "Oh please, can I keep her?" I whine to my husband. "I'll oil her and clean her and fill her little grease cups. Pleeeeeze?" In exchange, I usually do something rare and wonderful for him, like microwave him a potato for dinner. (A good marriage is full of give and take like that.)

I met a woman once who attracted Singer Feather-weights like flies (oooo, I've always hated that expression), but I don't seem to have that kind of luck. The machines that follow me home are heavy, frumpy, old green or beige things. Ah, but if those wonderful old girls could talk. They would tell me of the baby quilts, the Easter dresses, the high school graduation gowns, the polyester double-knit leisure suits, and of the women who used and loved them.

Let's face it, our tools are part of our passion. We owe it to ourselves to buy quality tools so we can love the process of quilting just as much as the finished result. And quality tools last and last and can be passed from generation to generation. When my son grows up, he will have children of his own . . . and he better keep them away from my good scissors.

The Naming of Quilts

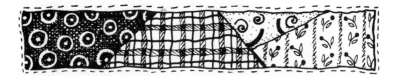

One of the highlights of any quilt show is to read the little placards next to each quilt on display. Sometimes there are histories or dedications; sometimes the little placards explain what was going on in the quilter's mind when he/she made the quilt. Sometimes there are no stories, just an enigmatic name such as "Transitions VI" or "Reflections." Some people are very practical with their names and tell it like it is: "Really Cute Skunks with Red and Pink Hearts."

I wonder how this naming of quilts got started. I don't think pioneer women named their quilts, did they? Oh, they might have referred to them as "Pink Ohio Star" and such, but I think that the naming of quilts must be a recent invention. We must have borrowed the naming of quilts from the naming of fine art.

My theory is that people who worked in museums must have been the first people to give names to works of art. I think they got tired of leaning off ladders with nails in their mouth and saying, "Hey, Giuseppi . . . hand me that square one over there. No, not that one, the one where the woman is smiling . . . no, not that woman, the other one, with the brown dress. Not that brown dress, the one with the . . . " and so on. It was so much easier to lean over and yell, "Hey Giuseppi! Toss me up the Mona Lisa!" And so a tradition was born.

I think naming a quilt is cheating. I think a person should have to look at a quilt and decide what it is without any help from a name on a placard. Not that you get much help from some placards; some are pretty vague. A "Transition" from what? I ask myself. "Reflections" of what? And which skunks are the "Really Cute" ones?

Furthermore, I believe that naming a quilt is cheating because with some imagination, a name can get a quilt into a themed show where it really doesn't belong at all. For instance, you have just completed a charm quilt consisting of 23,000 brown and blue triangles. A quilt show then announces that they will be accepting quilts into a show, the theme of which is to be "A Quilter's Garden." Now soccer season is fast approaching, so you know you won't have any time between running carloads of children out to pizza to translate Monet's Water Garden at Giverny into fabric. What will you do with your brown and blue triangle quilt?

Why, think of a name, of course. How about "Impressions of Periwinkles in a Field"? Or "Earth and Sky in Upheaval"? Or maybe "Compost in Space"? The more twisted your mind is, the better your chances. I don't think we should be rewarding this kind of behavior, do you?

I think that quilt names should remain neutral, like people names attempt to be. When you name a child William, he can grow up to be any kind of William he wants. No judgments are placed upon him until he goes out in the world and is judged by each individual he meets. At that point, by his own virtues, he can become easy-going Billy, straight-faced William, or that-idiot Bill. (There are a few names that, unfortunately, are not inherently neutral and may shadow public opinion unfairly, e.g. "Arnold," a name that sounds like someone gargling and is sure to produce a nervous, myopic child.)

So I recommend that we take our naming tradition from the naming of children instead of the naming of art. This way, you could show your quilts to people and they could form their own ideas of what your work means to them. You could say, "Edna, have you met my quilt, 'Rapunzel'?" Edna could then judge what kind of personality "Rapunzel" has. She could do this on visiting days at Happy Acres, right after she calls those nice men in white coats to come and get you.

Another idea is to allow a loved one to name the quilt for you. Some of the best names come from loved ones that own one of your quilts, especially very young children. It is a great honor when one of your quilts becomes a beloved "Ta-ta," or "Ba-blik" or some other highly improbable combination of syllables. Don't look for these names on museum or quilt-show placards though, as Ta-tas and Ba-bliks do not end up in those places. They usually end up in the garage or in bed with George and Bill, the miniature dachshunds. George and Bill, while experts in softness and warmth, have no respect for art and will shred and chew equally on a "Ba-blik," "Rapunzel," or "Transitions VI."

I hope I have given you some things to think about when you name your next beloved quilt. You are not obligated to name your quilt something poetic and transcendental; you can name it "Ernie" if you feel like it. After all, life at Happy Acres isn't so bad . . . that is, if I can only keep George and Bill away from "Rapunzel."

The Rusty Ol' Tractor Ruse

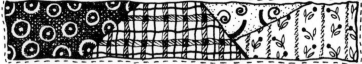

I remember the candy store when I was a kid. There was such an incredible variety of delectable delights in every shape and color. The candies were mostly individually wrapped and displayed in large stacked glass bins that reached high above my head. A quarter meant that I could have the candy-store clerk running around for at least 20 minutes, dipping into each brightly colored bin and filling my little bag with one of each flavor. My favorites were the green sour apple hard candies and those little pastel dots that came stuck on a paper roll.

The candy store was a magical place, a piece of heaven on earth. I can't say for sure, but I think this is where my love of shopping first began. Thirty-five years later, I still get this candy-store feeling every time I enter a quilt shop, only now, instead of lemon drops and licorice pastels, beautiful, multi-colored fat quarters are my weakness. And books, I love books. Tools, too. Oh, hey, I love it all. Unfortunately, I am not the queen of self-control. I haven't even visited the king-dom.

The only trouble, you see, is my husband. It isn't that he doesn't want me to have fabric, tools, and books (and scissors—did I mention scissors? I love scissors.). It's that I feel guilty buying all this stuff for myself. He sets such a good example for the family budget—always foregoing personal luxuries, making do with what he already has, building up the savings account instead of spending. He's just so disgustingly practical about everything.

So, yes, I am one of those people who used to feel compelled to sneak quilting stuff past my husband. It's not that he would get angry at all, I just didn't want to have to answer "the question." Do you know "the question" I'm talking about? Oh dear, I hate to even repeat it but here it is: "What are you going to use that for?" AAARRRRRGH. Oh, that was painful.

That question was agonizing on so many levels. First of all, I had to admit to my very practical hus-band that I had no idea what I was going to use this or that particular fabric for. And all the stuff that came out of my mouth after that sounded so frivolous to someone so practical. "I just might need it . . . uh, for something . . . .someday . . . I don't exactly know yet, but it will be just perfect for . . . uh . . . some-thing that I haven't . . . that I may . . . " And so I squirmed.

He even used to ask me "the question" every time I completed a quilt. I would put the last stitch in the binding, pick the stray threads off it, and wave my completed work of art around proudly in front of my husband. Then he would ask "the question." "What are you going to use that one for?" AAARRRRGH. I used to be able to use the excuse that we needed them to keep us warm, but after I had made at least 33 quilts for each bed in the house, I had to think of something else. Wall quilts were especially difficult to make sound practical: "The wall was cold"? I think not.

I wish I could have simply explained that some things don't necessarily have a function, that they are just wonderful to look at and touch and you just have to have them. But I tried that tactic many times, including once with the family pet. "It's a pet, dear. It doesn't have a function. You give it a name and then you feed it and comb it and take it to the vet when it is sick and clean up after it. What does it *do*? It doesn't really do anything but bark and shed and chew things up. You are just supposed to love it." AAARRRRGH. See what I am up against? You can't explain the function of a non-functional thing to practical person. They just don't get it.

One day, and I don't know what got into me, I tried to explain to my husband about how wonderful the quilt shop was and how difficult it was to avoid temptation there. For some weird reason, he assumed that I meant that I actually *wanted* to avoid temptation, and so he proceeded to give me a lecture on the correct way to shop, which I will recount here for your amusement. First, he makes a list. Each item on the list has been carefully considered as to its merits and drawbacks. He keeps the list for at least three weeks to make sure that he didn't put anything on there because of some wild impulsive whim (for example, who needs band-aids when you have duct tape?).

When he is absolutely sure he cannot do without an item, he picks a day of the week when no one else would ever be caught dead shopping, like a Sunday morning at seven a.m. Armed with his list, he clenches his jaw and enters the store. Taking care not to look around lest something tempt him, he marches straight to the item he needs, procures it, and proceeds directly to the cashier. He doesn't even glance at the magazines, candy bars, lint brushes, and novelty pens while in the checkout line. He pays for his item, catalogs his receipt, places his change in his wallet right side up in proper monetary sequence, and proceeds directly to his vehicle for the return trip home. All the way home, he contemplates the sad capitalistic nature of mankind. (Yes, I will accept fat quarters in lieu of sympathy cards.)

After I listened to this pitiful lecture, my eyes wide with horror (poor man!), I realized that his was a soul crying out in need of a little impulse-buying enlightenment. What he needed was some candy-store therapy.

I formed a plan. The following Saturday morning, I innocently requested that he accompany me to a yard sale (any yard sale would be fine). When we arrived at the yard sale, I scouted out the biggest, heaviest, ugliest, rustiest, spider-webbiest object with gears that I could find. "Wow, look at this ol' thing," I said. "Gee, I bet this ol' thing really used to run great. What a fine machine this must have been in its time! Why I'll bet it would run circles around a modern one of whatever this thing is. But who on earth could get this ol' thing running again . . . ?"

I no longer feel guilty about my trips to the fabric store since the day Mr. Rusty accompanied us home from the yard sale. Only trouble is, Mr. Rusty turned out to be quite a gregarious soul and invited his oxidized friends and relatives to take up residence in our garage and spew their various corroded entrails all over the garage floor. To me, it looks like a bunch of junk, but to my enlightened husband (the one over there with the sheepish grin), it's a beautiful candy-store dream come true.

Quilting Outlaw

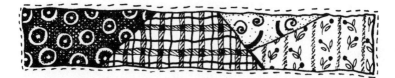

Let me start out by saying that I am basically a good, law-abiding citizen. I firmly believe in a set of written laws that allows us to live together peacefully in society. I pay my taxes, drive the speed limit, and do not take more than my share of the little round soup crackers from the restaurant basket. I don't even take the hotel shampoo home with me.

But I have a dark confession to make: when it comes to quilting, I am an uncivilized barbarian, an unrepentant renegade. I follow no rules. I am a quilting outlaw. Color wheel? Ha! I laugh at the laws of physics. Perfectly pointy points? Who needs 'em? Tiny little micro-stitches? Don't even think about it. (Note: To be really effective, these last few sentences need to be said aloud in your best Clint Eastwood impersonation.)

It isn't that I can't follow these rules. I just don't understand why they exist in the first place. Who made such rules, anyway? Why do we consider some characteristics of a quilt admirable and others detestable?

That Dorky Homemade Look

(I'm sure someone has probably written a book on this somewhere, but I'm too lazy to read it, and facts would only confuse my opinion anyway.) I'm sure these rules came about when quilting was considered "only" a craft and not an art form. But now that we have come to appreciate quilts as art, let's pay them the ultimate homage and drop the rules. Imagine telling Van Gogh that his Sunflowers were not pointy enough! No wonder artists go mad. Liberate quilts from the tyranny of standards! Let them be free from artificial constraints!

But wait. Before you grab your picket sign and write your congressperson, I'm talking about this revolution on a personal level, in your own sewing room. Do you follow the rules because you like the results, or do you follow the rules because you are afraid of the Quilt Police? Oh, you know who I mean. They're everywhere, in your guilds and mini-groups. They're the silent types with the pursed lips and the disdainful looks. As a matter of fact, at this very moment, they are convened in a secret session to discuss that wonky seam in your last quilt.

Do you quilt to please them? Are you afraid to bring an imperfect work to show because someone may whisper about your set-in corners? Don't be afraid! The Quilt Police are imaginary! The overwhelming majority of your fellow quilters are loving and accepting and feel very honored that you bring your work to share. They cherish your imagination, not your six-way seams.

Consider the following situations. What if I told you that I would give you a quilt that is technically perfect in every way? It has 3,000 pointy points, is quilted 24 stitches to the inch, and has an incredible 4,000 tiny stuffed berries on the surface. It hangs straight and true and it has won several awards, and I am going to give it to you to hang in your living room. Sound good? It's yours.

Too bad it won those awards in 1970 and is constructed from burnt orange, avocado green, and earth-brown, polyester double-knit fabric. (It was made from the discarded leisure suits of aluminum siding salesmen.) Will you still hang it in a place of honor in your living room?

On the other hand, imagine being a slave in the days before the Civil War. You have only homespun scraps, rusty scissors, thread salvaged from your master's old clothing, and no straight-edge to boot. You make a quilt that, 100 years later, becomes a national treasure and hangs in a museum, worshiped by millions. Now, who followed the rules and who didn't? Did the rules matter?

Rules are temporal and fleeting; time itself forgives violations of the Quilt Penal Codes. Amnesty is eventually bestowed on even the lowliest. Brace yourself: future quilt museums could be full of yarn-tied polyester comforters because, we all know, they will never biodegrade.

So, where did I put the point of this narrative anyway? Oh, here it is: enjoy the process. Don't worry about judgments, and realize that the rules are something you can embrace or reject at will, whatever suits you. Quilting styles, fabric colors, opinions, and rules change with time. The only truly lasting thing in a quilt is the love you sew into it.

As for me, I love to torment the Quilt Police every chance I get. I guess there's no hope for incorrigibles like me. I'll probably end up in Quilt Jail someday, being forced to stuff tiny little harvest-gold polyester berries for the rest of my life. Come to think of it, I may just turn myself in—I hear that I'm wanted by the Cooking Police. Talk about cruel and unusual punishment . . .

My
Next Quilt

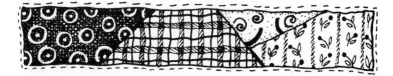

For me, the most exciting time in quiltmaking is contemplating my next project. Since I like to make only one quilt at a time, I usually collect new ideas that appeal to me for future quilts while I am still working on a current project.

I start with an empty manila folder, and I fill it with pictures torn out of magazines, photos or mementos that I want to commemorate, or maybe a story, poem, or phrase that will shape the mood of my next quilt. Then when it comes time to actually start the new quilt, I look in the folder, pick out an idea or combination of ideas, and go with it.

This morning, as I was finishing up the binding on a scrappy Christmas Sawtooth Star, I was eagerly anticipating having a cup of tea and looking through the ideas I had collected during the past month. As I had just made 324 scrappy red and green stars, I knew that I never wanted to see another Christmas print for the rest of my life. (I got to where I was taking more pleasure than I should have in whacking little dancing snowmen to pieces with my rotary cutter.) I wanted to make something really different this time. So here I sit with my cup of herbal tea. Let's open up this folder and see what ideas I have for my next project . . .

This time my folder is full of fun ideas that I've collected. The first idea here on top is a bat block (yes, as in vampires, etc.) that I designed for a Halloween quilt. As I was designing the block, I was saddened to observe that the only time bats ever get made into quilts is at Halloween, and then only rarely. Furthermore, bats are usually lowly players in a Halloween scene, barely noticeable next to colorful, frolicking scarecrows and jolly, orange pumpkins. This is an inexcusable lapse on our part.

Bats are marvelous animals, because it just so happens that bats can consume about 5,000 bugs *each* day. That's 5,000 less spiders jumping out at you in the shower, 5,000 less earwigs slithering out at you from underneath your houseplants. Why is it then that we are reluctant to honor these humble heroes in our quilts?

I believe this oversight must be due solely to a design problem. Bats, you see, are black—and they only come out at night. This situation presents us with an unfortunate lack of contrast from an artistic standpoint. Therefore, in order to pay homage to the underappreciated bat, I have decided to remedy the situation by solving this design dilemma. I think I'll make the bats in pastels, or maybe cheery tropical brights, swooping out of confetti-laden, blue skies, perhaps dive-bombing a few insufferably smug pumpkins.

What else do I have in here? Oh, I love this idea. It is a picture that I tore out of a mail-order catalog that came unrequested in the mail. (I figure if they send me a catalog that I didn't ask for, I can steal any ideas out of it that I want.) It's a picture of a fringed wool throw with yellow bananas on it. The bananas looked like they were tossed onto it by some angry chimp, the bananas facing this way and that. I like it because it looks so festive, like an impromptu banana party.

You know, it just occurred to me that you never see bananas on quilts, except for maybe one or two igno-miniously stuffed into a fruit arrangement. Bananas are never the stars; they seem always to be peeking out from behind grapes or some other fruit considered more respectable. I should make a banana quilt. Hey, that gives me an idea. I'll make a quilt with bats *and* bananas. That will be great. I'll just alternate blocks and . . . . hey wait, here's another idea . . . .

This idea is a very special and meaningful one to me. This is my son's name spelled out in noodles and beans. There are noodles in every shape and size, and beans of many varieties. He even put a little wagon-wheel noodle at the end of his name for a period. Wow, that's cute.

I remember the day I picked him up at school and he was clutching this in his hand. He was beaming with pride as he showed me his noodle name. I think it was the look on his face that really got to me, the joy of having his name enshrined forever in pasta. Oh, I just have to use this idea, too. I could applique his name or one of his poems in nice little macaroni shapes.

Okay, what do we have so far? A bat, banana, bean and noodle quilt. I can really start to see it, a few pieced bats, some appliqued food and . . .

Oh, wait. I just have to do this one, too. It's a fabric chicken that I've been saving. I made it after reading about a party game where you give all the participants some blank construction paper and a pair of scissors and have them cut out the shape of an elephant. The best elephant wins the prize. The only catch is that the participants must accomplish this task while wearing a blindfold. At the end of the game, the contestants are un-blindfolded and the various misshapen elephants are demonstrated. Hilarity ensues. (No wonder I never go to parties.)

This idea appealed to me because my drawing skills seem to constantly compromise my applique work. If I could bypass the drawing and go straight to cutting, I figure I might fare better. So in the privacy of my own home one day, I picked out a rag from my dust-rag bin (no sense in wasting my good fabric scraps) and tried to imagine an elephant. I closed my eyes and commenced snipping. When I opened my eyes, I couldn't believe it. There in my hands was the most perfect chicken I'd ever seen. I just had to save it to applique to something. I only wish I hadn't cut it out of my husband's old boxer shorts. Oh well, no one will notice. So now I have a bat, banana, bean, elephant-chicken . . . uh, what else was I going to put on here? Oh yes, noodles.

Any other good ideas in here? Oh well, I better stop at this point. Having too much to look at on a quilt is not a good idea, artistically speaking. I mean, I wouldn't want it to look tacky or anything now, would I?

Quilters, Sharks, and Modern Plastics

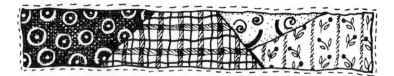

When I was a young college student, I was invited to my first "plastic-container-that-burps" party. (I can't use the trademark name here, but use your imagination.) I thought my neighbor was toying with me when she first described what the party was about, but I went anyway.

At first, it seemed like most of the bridal showers I had attended. But after the little pink and green mints were passed around, a somewhat prim and bespectacled plastic-container lady stood up in front of the crowd and began her speech. The room fell silent as she held up each piece of colorful molded plastic, and with great reverence, described in immense detail all the marvelous things you could place in those plastic containers if you wanted to. There were hot-dog holders and pickle-grabbers and deviled-egg keepers; there were shrimp-salad molds and doggie-kibble bins. The more she extolled the virtues of each little plastic miracle, the more I realized how impoverished my life had been up to that point.

Quilters, Sharks, and Modern Plastics

Here I was, thinking it was my youth or lack of self-assurance that had been keeping me from reaching true fulfillment, when it was really a food containment system problem. And apparently the rest of the room felt the same way, for when the pencils were passed out, the buying fury began. A few weeks later, as I sat in the living room staring at my plastic taco-storage unit, I wondered what had happened to all of us. How did that innocent-looking, plastic-container lady whip us up into a buying frenzy like that? And what was I ever going to do with this plastic pickle-picker I purchased?

So what does my pickle-picker have to do with quilting? Well, have you ever gone fabric shopping with a quilt friend and ended up with fabrics you would have never bought if you went alone? She might have led you to a rack of fabrics that you had never looked at before, or perhaps to a part of the store that you usually don't venture into. Then she probably gravitated to a particular bolt of fabric that you never would have noticed in a million years and, with abject enthusiasm, started listing all of its wonderful possibilities. Before you knew it, that fabric started to look pretty good, didn't it? As a matter of fact, you became almost certain that without a piece of that fabric, the rest of your life would not have been worth living. So you bought a yard or six.

Let me give you a tardy piece of advice at this point. Next time, just throw it out the car window on the way home. You will never use it. You have become a victim of the Plastic Container Phenomenon.

Having been a lifelong victim of this contagious malady myself, I have studied it extensively. ("Studied it extensively" means that I have thrown a lot of things out the window on my way home.) Enthusiasm is contagious, whether it be for Press 'n Store Hamburger Patty Keepers or fabric. I know, because I have personally witnessed a busload of quilters, fueled by each other's enthusiasm, descend upon a quilt shop and nearly empty it in seconds flat.

Have you ever seen one of those underwater documentaries about sharks? Here's what happens. First, they lower this diver down into the ocean in this itty-bitty cage with bars on it that look like they're spaced way too far apart for my thinking. And then the diver guy inside the cage starts waving these disgusting fish parts around. Then, out of nowhere, these quilters come on this bus trip, see, and . . . oh wait . . . I'm mixing up my examples. Oh well, you get my drift.

I, myself, have been accused of spreading excessive enthusiasm around. At one time, I worked in a wonderful quilt shop in Kauai. The shop itself was (and still is!) a historical landmark, charming as anything, and filled to the brim with gorgeous fabrics, especially brightly-colored tropical prints.

When a customer would approach the cutting table with a bolt of fabric and the store was sufficiently full of people, I would take the opportunity to spread some real enthusiasm. I would imagine myself as the plastic-container lady of fabric as I hammed it up at the cutting table. "This fabric you've selected is divine!" I would say loudly to the customer, making sure that the rest of the crowded store would hear my broadcast. "This fabric would look gorgeous in a quilt!" Using my best Vanna White poses, I would pat it and drape it and wave it around.

Customers would begin to peer out from behind bolts of fabric to see what I was going on about. "And wouldn't it be stunning made up with these coordinating fabrics!" Wandering over slowly, a crowd would build around the table, discreetly trying to get a better look. "Can't you just picture all these fabrics made up into a breathtaking Courthouse Steps?" By then, a mob had assembled, elbowing each other to get a better look. I would wait until the time was just right . . . and then . . . toss out the fish parts: "Gee, there isn't much fabric left on these bolts. You'd better grab several yards while you can." Poof. Fabric-feeding frenzy.

I like to think those customers eventually found a use for those wonderful fabrics that I schmoozed them into. Perhaps I broadened a few palettes, expanded some concepts, made fellow quilters aware of some new possibilities. If not, I'd love to follow that bus and catch all that fabric flying out the windows.

The Quilting Lecture Circuit

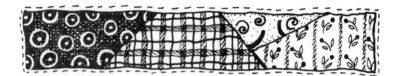

Brrrring. "Hello?"

"Hi. Is this Lisa Boyer? Good. This is the Symposium of Quilters Unified In Sewing Happiness (SQUISH). We would like to invite you and your sister to come speak at our third annual convention."

"Maybe . . . what's in it for me?"

"How about the respect and admiration of your peers, doughnuts, the knowledge that you are spreading the doctrine of quilting, and thereby furthering our cherished heritage, not to mention personal enlightenment, as well as contributing to history and the art of humankind?"

"Doughnuts? Did you say doughnuts?"

"We will arrange to pick you both up tonight. You will be flown to Yugoslavia in an ancient biplane by a circus acrobat. We will have to fly you in low at night to avoid radar detection. You will be speaking to 3,000 eastern European women who do not understand English. Your presentation will last for approximately eight hours, and, sorry, there are no restroom facilities."

"Gee, I don't know . . . what kind of doughnuts?

Unfortunately, when I get a guild or organization's phone call first, I know from experience that they have already tried to reach my sister and she wasn't home. Yes, I know that she has all the public-speaking ability in the family, is definitely the best teacher, makes the best quilts, and owns the projector. But just how good would she look teamed up next to someone who's actually competent? I serve as, well . . . contrast. That's why we are a successful team.

Brrrrrring. "Hello?"

"Hi Jane Ann, this is your sister Lisa. You feel like doing anything tonight? For instance, oh, I don't know . . . earning the respect and admiration of your peers, spreading the doctrine of quilting, and thereby further-ing our cherished heritage, personally enlightening yourself, contributing to the art of humankind? I'll pick you up as soon as it gets dark."

"Okay, sure . . . I just have to . . . hey, wait a minute. The last time you said those words we ended up in a Mexican jail trying to bribe the guards with our bodies. They never did stop laughing. Did someone offer you doughnuts again?"

I guess that's why they call her the smart one, too. But between misadventures, lecturing is an awesome and rewarding experience. The same lecture takes on a different tone and hue each time it is given, depending on variables such as type of audience, time of day, age group, gullibility, kind of doughnuts, etc.

I prefer lecturing in the afternoon. People wake up from your lecture feeling refreshed. And a really, really desperate audience is good. I recently lived on the tiny Hawaiian island of Kauai for six years, and I didn't travel much because flying is not my thing, to put it mildly. So any quilter we could lure there to come talk about quilting was met with open arms and endless poi (the Hawaiian equivalent of doughnuts. At least that's what we told the gullible lecturers. Boy, was it hard to keep a straight face sometimes.). But we were fortunate enough to get some wonderful quilters to come and lecture to us (at least until the poi thing got around), and it was thrilling.

I thank all those wonderful women who came out there to lecture to us and would like to let them know how much they contributed to my own unique lecture style. Unfortunately, they all declined having their names listed. I can't think why.

In conclusion, I want to encourage any of you interested in lecturing to pursue your dream. It is the most rewarding experience you can imagine, and the people you meet in your travels are simply the best on earth. See you in Yugoslavia and don't forget the doughnuts.

The Zen of Seam Ripping

As a teacher, I can't think of anything that sets off more negative emotion than suggesting that a participant rip out a seam and try it over again. I have spent many hours contemplating this phenomenon, and, as you can see, I plan to write a lengthy article on the psychology of seam ripping, as well as constructive ways in which to come to grips with the karmic seam-ripping experience. Hey, it won't be so bad. I once listened to Harriet Hargrave talk for two hours about *batting* and it was fascinating. Okay, so I'm not Harriet. But she's probably off doing something constructive right now, so you're gonna have to listen to me or finally get up and cook dinner, so what's it gonna be? I thought so.

Let us contemplate the physics of seam-ripping first. Don't you think that it is, at the very least, amazing that with this humble little tool, you can actually reverse the destructive, point-munching forces of the universe? You can go back, armed with your special little sword, and retrieve those little lost points out of those wicked seam allowances. And think of what a miracle it is, actually being able to travel back, back in time, to where you were before you spent those two hours matching 6,000 seams together, only to realize you sewed the two halves of your quilt together upside down. Just 18 hours with your seam ripper, and it's like the mistake never happened at all!

Ah, if there was only a seam ripper you could take to your life, huh? You could take out all the tacky parts and re-sew it seamlessly. And no one would ever know about that time you_____(complete this sentence yourself). Or think about being able to take a seam ripper to someone else's existence? Personally, there's this rusty old tractor fascination my husband could do very well without. Any failure or shortcoming you could imagine . . . rip, rip, rip! Out it comes. Sew a new perfect one in its place. A perfect universe for under a dollar.

One practical suggestion I have (and you better listen because you know I don't have many) is to replace your seam ripper often. It's my experience that the quilters who whine most piteously about having to rip something out are those quilters with horrible, dull, rusty rippers—I'm talking about something you actually need a tetanus shot in order to use. Treat yourself. They aren't that expensive, and what a difference a truly fine sharp one makes.

Now that you have a new seam ripper, take some time to make friends with it. Get used to the way it feels in your hand. Give it a name. My seam ripper's name is Jack. Jack the Ripper and I have a great relationship. He never reminds me of what a stupid thing I just did. He just leaps into my hand, ready to help me correct it. We are a team and I depend on him many times. Many, many times. But he never tells on me. What a guy.

How did I come upon this benign philosophy of seam-ripping, you may ask. I once made a big yellow king-size quilt. It was a cheery, multi-colored nosegay, set diagonally with alternating plain blocks. And it wasn't a comforter, mind you. It went all the way to the floor all the way around. I was temporarily living in Oregon at the time and couldn't possibly have quilted the incredibly large beast myself. Perpetually on a budget, I called around, looking for the cheapest price for someone to machine-quilt it for me.

Being fresh from a tiny isolated island, I thought everyone on the mainland was an expert about this. I found a lady to do it for me at an incredible price in just a couple of days, so I took my very large quilt to her. I should have turned around and run when she pointed out that I had cut all the outside edge triangles on the bias and she would "see what she could do."

True to her word, she finished it in record time and I picked it up that afternoon. She had it folded nicely so that the edges of the quilt were not visible at the time that I paid her. I left, feeling like I had gotten a really good deal. Later that night, I decided to start putting on the binding. I unfolded the quilt to measure around the edges and just about cried. For about 30 inches in, all the way around the periphery of the quilt, was the lumpiest, bumpiest mess you ever saw. I can hardly joke about it even now, it was so terrible. There were wrinkles sewn into it as big as three inches across.

I had a decision to make. I could fold the thing up and forget about it forever, or I could make peace with the universe and get into the zen of seam-ripping. I am happy to say that it graces my bed today, and I am very happy that I didn't give up on it. Thanks, Jack. You're a cosmic wonder.

A Great Quilting Truth of the Universe

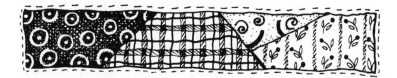

My sister called me long distance from her workplace between patients today. She had a pressing question that had been causing her to lose sleep. She wanted to know how I organize my fabric stash. As an avid beginner, she told me that she first had her small fabric collection organized into lights and darks, but now her stash had grown, and that system of organization was simply not sufficient anymore.

She asked me if I arranged my fabric collection by color wheel, you know, colors and their analogous counterparts on one shelf, complementary colors on the other. Or did I arrange the fabrics by cool colors versus warm colors? Or perhaps according to scale of print: separate stacks for large florals, small geometrics, and blenders? And how did I catalog amounts? Make tags? Keep a fabric journal?

As the experienced quilter in the family, I quickly tried to make up an answer. "Oh . . . yes . . . all those things work . . ." I stammered, daunted by her enthusiasm. I was glad at that point that she lived at the other end of California and couldn't see into my sewing room at that moment. "And don't forget to separate out the monochromatics from the polychromatics," I reminded her, not having the slightest idea what I meant.

After we hung up, a great Quilting Truth of the Universe suddenly came to me. (If nine more come to me, I promise to travel to the nearest mountaintop and write them all down on stone tablets.) This great Quilting Truth of the Universe is a simple one: each person has her (or his) own precious quilting personality which permeates every aspect of her (or his) art, from organization to execution to exhibition. And because each of us is unique, each quilt is beautifully and wondrously different. It's as if our souls were laid open and squashed down into every color and fiber of the thing. A quilt is a song, a dance, a soft soothing poem, or a tumultuous scream of panic. (Okay, maybe I am the only one who has ever made a tumultuous scream of panic quilt, but you get the idea.)

Yes, yes, yes, I know you have heard this all before, that each quilt is unique and individual, blah, blah, blah. I have, too. But do you really cherish your own quilting style? Do you love your own work, no matter what your mistakes are? Do you realize that your quilts symbolize the very essence of your personality? Can you look at your own quilting mistakes, regrets, misjudgments, and shortcomings, and give yourself permission to be proud of yourself? Can you look at yourself in the form of a quilt?

My sister and I are vastly different illustrations of the above truth. She conceives in her mind the exact quilt she would like to make, carefully selects fabric from the quilting shop, takes her choices home, and neatly folds, catalogs, and arranges her selections according to the color wheel. She then uses it as planned in a carefully executed color study. Her quilts show that she is creative, colorful, imaginative, and . . . well, beautiful.

On the other hand, let me tell you what happens to me. Since I am constantly on a budget, I can never afford more than a half-yard of anything. I go to the quilt shop and try to cover my ears and use my eyes only. I look at all the gorgeous fabric parading before me, like contestants at the Miss Universe Pageant. But the same thing always happens to me. It comes on slowly at first, somewhat subliminally, but it creeps slowly into my consciousness . . . there . . . did you hear that? A whimper? A tiny little plaintive cry emanating from the homely bolt at the back of the store? "Buy me and make me beautiful!" it cries. "Love me . . . nobody else will! If you don't buy me, I'll end up on the sale rack and be puckered and scrunched up forever in a . . . .gasp! . . . rag rug! Save meeeeee!"

"No!" I yell back. "Pick on someone else! I saved all your ugly brothers and sisters! Leave me alone!"

"Appreciate me! Showcase me! Make me into a quilt!" it whines pitifully.

I never win this fight, though. I own the Humane Society of Fabric. And with all that, you'd think that the fabric would be grateful. But it isn't. Once I get it home and put it on the shelf with the other fabrics, they all wait until I am out of the room. Then they prowl and roam like beasts. They tear big pieces out of each other. They mate and create little genetic mutants of fabric that I swear I didn't buy. Worst of all, when I try to use them in a quilt, they get really ugly. They conspire to vibrate and glow and wander all over the place, losing their little points in the process.

And this is precisely what fascinates me about quilting. If I could control and tame the fabrics, I think I might get bored. But the fabrics continue to surprise and thrill me. They have their own personalities. They leap and contort and complain, and somehow I talk them down and settle them into a quilt. My mistakes are most often better than my best-laid plans.

But I didn't tell any of this to my sister. Her life is as well planned and structured as her gorgeous quilts are, and the organization of her stash will be another aspect of her quilting style that makes her unique.

And frankly, she thinks I'm weird enough without having to hear that fabric talks to me. I won't tell her either that I wrap myself up in my own artwork and giggle out loud, pleased as punch in what I have created. But I'll bet you anything that she does exactly the same thing.

Beauty
and the Beast

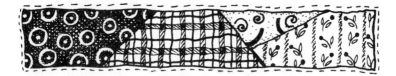

"There she is . . . Miss Beeeyoou-teeee-fulllll . . . "
the emcee would sing, voice quivering with emotion,
flagellating his free arm about in broad, expansive ges-
tures.

Meanwhile, the newly crowned and sobbing Miss
Beautiful America would wobble unsteadily down the
catwalk atop her four-inch high heels. A 300-pound
ermine-trimmed cape constricting her windpipe, and
clutching a giant bouquet of red roses to her chest, she
would struggle to keep her head erect so that her
rhinestone tiara would not topple from her head and
go scudding off into the audience. Blinded by tears and
hobbled, she would miraculously ambulate to the end
of the runway and pause so that thousands of flashbulbs would have the opportunity to further impair her
vision by barbecuing their red blobby imprints into her
corneas.

Turning back to the ever-singing emcee (who by this
time was making up verses), she would navigate

blindly upstage again—past the twirled puddle of cape at her feet, past the furiously snapping flashbulbs, past the gawking crowd, all the while smiling through the stabbing pain of 24 long-stemmed red-rose thorns embedding themselves into her chest.

Ah . . . and all this glory awarded for just a few short years spent living on nothing but grapefruit rinds and orthodontic wax.

I've always held a morbid fascination for beauty contests. Being born without a competitive bone in my body, I can't understand why women go through all of that. No matter how perfect your body, can you imagine having to compare your thighs to thousands of other perfect thighs? Imagine how a hundredth of an inch waistline difference, or one tiny fat dimple on your behind, would send you plunging into the deep abyss of despair!

I think each of us should now pause for a moment in order to reflect on and be grateful for any of our body parts that have rescued us from this fate. I have my ankles to thank. My friend Kathy tells me that they look a lot like Fred Flintstone's. My legs come down to where my ankles should be and just sort of bend unceremoniously into a foot shape. Thank you, ankles, for saving me from the tortured life of a beauty-queen contestant. Thank you, upper arms. Thank you, thighs. Thank you . . . no wait, that's quite enough.

That Dorky Homemade Look

Since I have admitted to this deep-seated anxiety about competition, you can imagine my fear of entering my quilts into quilt shows. Just the thought of one of my poor, homemade quilts hanging there among the other perfect thighs—uh . . . I mean, quilts—makes me perspire around the waistband. But at the same time, I love *going* to quilt shows. I can't imagine what would happen if everyone would ninny out of them like I try to.

I guess I can blame my angst on watching too many beauty pageants. How can they possibly pick one perfect perfect woman out of all those excruciatingly perfect women? Actually, I know how—they put all of those perfect women up on one stage standing right next to each other. Soon, you start to notice that perhaps Miss Podunk's feet are bigger that anyone else's. And look at that . . . Miss Piddletown's nose isn't quite as straight as the other 49 noses, is it? The tiniest imperfections are hideously magnified. Comparison is a painful thing!

This being the case, do I really want to hang one of my dorky, homemade quilts next to hundreds of other beautiful quilts at a quilt show? Aaaaaauuugh! Mine would look like Winston Churchill in a bathing suit and high heels.

Incredible as it seems to me, some quilters actually thrive on competition. My sister had the courage to enter her very first quilt in a quilt competition. My first quilt, on the other hand, was immediately buried on my son's bed, back side up and three layers down. I am terrified when he doesn't make his bed because someone might actually see it. I'm surprised it doesn't give him nightmares. It is a horrid blue and brown ordeal in log-cabin form; I made it in my first quilting class.

I distinctly remember the teacher of the class, who took pictures of every quilt in the class for her photo album—except mine. She kindly extended her sympathy at the end of the class and assured me that not everyone gets it right the first time. Well that's okay, I thought, noting that my thighs were slightly smaller than hers. (I guess cattiness goes hand-in-hand with defeat.)

Despite all my fears, I do manage to work up the courage to put one of my quilts in a quilt show every year. (I keep hoping that someday some quilt show will offer a "Miss Congeniality" award category.) Every time I enter, I think about how thankful I am for the people who actually *like* to compete and therefore make quilt shows the delightful events that they are. I also remember to breathe a silent thank-you to quilt show chickens like me who are there only because they know that without quilts, there can be no quilt show. Above all, when I am lucky enough to attend one of these marvelous events, I make a special point to appreciate the quilts like mine—the quilts with big feet and crooked teeth and funny hair. We're all beautiful!

It's A Flat World
After All

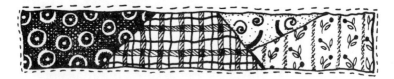

Okay, sometimes I feel like I complain too much. I consider myself a very positive person, but some things just really get to me, you know? Like why do they make diet salad dressing so slimy? It's like eating a salad that an army of giant slugs has oozed across. Uh-oh, there I go again. I guess I should make some sort of resolution to reserve my complaints for the really big stuff. For instance, the structure of the universe. I think we have far too many dimensions, don't you?

Since I am a fan of science magazines, I read articles all the time about new dimensions being discovered, or at least theorized. I don't remember how many there are at last count, and, frankly, I don't want to know. The very thought of all those dimensions out there makes me want to take my Dramamine and head straight for bed. Why do we need all these dimensions anyway?

For all of you persons that didn't pay attention in physics class (me included), two dimensions are what straight, flat things are—kind of like a quilt with a low-loft batting. I am a big fan of the first two dimensions. If you and I were two-dimensional, we could be thin in at least one direction. But that third dimension! That's where things get confusing. The third dimension gives shape and depth to our world. It means that you must remember which way to turn when you come out of the kitchen in order to find the sewing room. It also means you can make quilts of varying thicknesses, which is just about the only thing the third dimension is good for.

Yes, I know I'm being a little bit negative about the third dimension, but it's tortured me my whole life. I can remember being a little girl in elementary school, taking my first IQ test. I sailed through the spelling, grammar, math, and science questions with ease. I was feeling happy and confident, just breezing along figuring out if Dick and Jane were running or had already run. But at the end of the intelligence test, there were two pages of these . . . things . . . that stopped me dead in my tracks! There, on the last two pages, were some horribly convoluted, three-dimensional figures that you were supposed to inspect carefully, turn around in your brain, and decide which multiple-choice figure most closely matched the theoretical back side of the pointy mangled blob in the example.

Were they kidding? How was I supposed to know what that blob looked like on the other side? How did they know it had another side, and, if they were so interested in it, why didn't they just draw that side instead? I sat struggling with these very questions when the timer sounded, ending the test, and I hadn't even figured out the first blob! I was devastated. If being able to think in three dimensions was a sign of intelligence, how would I ever survive? How would I ever get a job? And what kind of sandwich did my mom pack in my lunch today anyway? (Attention span has never been my strong suit either.)

To this day, I can blame all sorts of things on my lack of 3D ability. I have no spatial perception and no idea what the back side of anything looks like. You have never seen anyone as inept as I am in picking out furniture for a room. It's always too big, too small, or has to be divided between two rooms. I frequently get lost in malls, can never find my car in a parking lot, and my meringue always collapses (okay, that last one is weak, but things are rolling for me).

I can't sew dresses either. Dresses are three-dimensional. I do not understand them. Take set-in sleeves, for instance. How can you possibly attach that giant sleeve tube at a 90 degree angle onto that tiny armhole tube? And the pattern tries to talk you into attempting this hopeless task by calling it "ease." Ha! I think it should be called, "Hard! Very very hard!" Match point A to point B indeed!

So you can certainly understand how my interest in

sewing came to be focused solely on traditional quilt-making. Traditional quilts are a blessing: square blocks, straight lines, and low-loft batting fit magically together into a soothing symphony of two-dimensional loveliness.

Since I discovered quilting 12 years ago, I have only strayed from the straight and narrow once. During a weak moment, I was seduced by a class sample of a gorgeous quilt, flowing with oodles of long, graceful curves that swirled around each other like boiling spaghetti noodles. Forgetting my history (I told you my attention span was short), I signed up for the quilt class. I knew I was in trouble when the teacher claimed that the curves were as easy as doing a set-in sleeve. Well, maybe a thousand set-in sleeves. After many hours of total frustration, my tiny quilt top of a thousand set-in curves looked like a relief map of the Swiss Alps. It was lumpy and bumpy and curled into a shape much like an armadillo protecting itself. After I finally located my car in the parking lot, I returned home and vowed never to curve again.

I guess I have already broken my resolution not to complain anymore. I'm sorry, it's just that the third dimension has always been a sore spot with me. I don't have anything against the rest of the dimensions, mainly because I don't know what they are. I think the fourth dimension may have something to do with time, but I'm not sure. I believe the fifth dimension was a singing group in the 60's. The sixth dimension must have something to do with cooking, which explains why it's so totally beyond my comprehension.

As for the rest of the dimensions, I think that they're a terrible waste of space and time. And I think physicists should just stop worrying about dimensions and apologize for torturing little school children who are so upset about blobs that they can't remember what kind of sandwich they brought in their lunches. As for set-in sleeves, well, I don't want to complain, but . . .

Blame
the Quilt

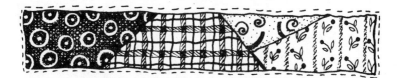

Many people ask me about my design process. "How did you get the idea for this quilt?" they ask. Well, actually, the question comes out more like, "How on earth did you ever come up with this thing?" but I know what they mean. Unfortunately, I can never think up a brilliant response . . . uh, I mean answer . . . quickly enough. I wish I could claim to have drawn up a diagram, hand-painted my own fabrics, and obtained a vision for the quilting pattern while on a spiritual trek through the Himalayas.

To be truthful, I am afflicted with over-eagerness when it comes to my fabric and rotary cutter. My artistic vision only goes as far as "What fabric do I feel like cutting up today?" Usually I reach into my scrap bag and find something already in shreds that deserves hacking up. (My "good" stash is so nicely folded and intact that I can't bear to use it.)

I generally select a block pattern from a decaying pattern book I picked up at a yard sale for a nickel.

Matching rotting pattern to tattered fabric, I go for it. The quilt has begun.

If I happen to like the block I have made, I make more of them. If, on the other hand, I didn't enjoy making the block (for instance, too many set-in corners makes me queasy), I make a different block, and my quilt immediately becomes a sampler quilt.

How big should I make it? Hmmmm, that depends on my attention span that particular day. Finally, when I am finished making all the blocks I want to, I pin the blocks up on my design wall and wait for the quilt to talk to me.

The trouble with waiting for a quilt to talk to you is that sometimes you have to wait for a while. For instance, I made a quilt top out of 56 scrappy Christmas Sawtooth Stars back in November. Here it is February, and I am still staring at it. What does it want? Sometimes I think it's very clearly whispering "applique border!" at me. Then it will visit me in a dream in the form of a big puffy cloud and tell me very clearly that it wants a Nine-Patch border. Other times it will sneak up on me when I am at my computer thinking about something else entirely and startle me by yelling, "FLYING GEESE!" over my shoulder. Honestly, I don't think that quilt will ever make up its mind.

A scrap quilt is like that, you know. All those different fabrics just can't agree on anything. The blocks fight until you have to either separate them with sash-ing or bind them together with a strong border. It's all the quilt's fault, you see, not mine. If it can't decide what it wants, how should I know?

Yes, I do envy those quilters with a plan who don't have to be bossed around by their unfinished quilts. I am amazed when some quilt artists even go so far as to draw out a picture in advance! Ow! It's enough to make my brain hurt. I hate decisions. I avoid them until they are unavoidable, which is why my Christmas quilt is still staring at me in February.

I've thought about taking my quilt into the fabric shop and letting it pick out its own border, but quilt shop owners get nervous if you stand around trying to reason with your quilt top about coming to some sort of decision. Besides, the quilt could choose to have one of its silent spells, which means that I would have to be responsible for looking through roughly 2,000 bolts of fabric and having to rule out 1,999 of them. How could I possibly make 1,999 decisions in one day? Ow! Ow! My brain hurts again.

Okay, I realize I'm a little bit decision-challenged. My friends don't share my decision-making problem. They welcome choices—they practically thrive on them. Not only do they regularly patrol every fabric shop within a hundred mile radius, they send away for mail-order swatches. Some find new and exciting fabric on the internet. And, as if 60,000 fabric choices aren't enough, they sign up for fabric-dying, -painting, and -printing classes so that they can have 80,000 choices! Ow! Ow! Where's the aspirin?

You must admit that the number of quilting choices available has become staggering. Not only do you have to choose fabric color and style, you have to choose pattern, thread, batting, technique, gadget types, plain or peanut M&M's . . . the list is endless. And just when you comfortably make up your mind forever that you will never ever have to consider using that disgusting baby by-product green fabric, one of your friends makes a quilt from that very fabric that knocks your socks off. Poof! Another hard-earned, carefully considered decision blown to bits.

When you put all the factors together, it seems easier to rely on talking quilts than artistic vision. As a matter of fact, I consider the short-attention span type of quilting that I do . . . well, it's sort of an adventure. I never know what will happen and what I will end up with. Of course, if it turns out admirably, I'll claim that I planned it that way. And if it doesn't turn out nicely, it's not my fault. It's the quilt's fault.

The Third One Back on the Right

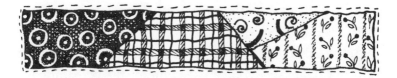

There exists an old saying that "the best idea is always the third one back." In other words, if you have three ideas lined up in your brain, the third one you thought of is probably the best idea. I guess the brain works a lot like I do when I make pancakes. I never seem to get the first two pancakes to come out right. The first pancake is always underdone with unattractive batter blebs flowing out of it. The second pancake is usually burned because I've turned the heat up too much after the first under-done one. But the third pancake! Perfectly sized, admirably poured, and skillfully flipped—a monument to pancake loveliness. (Meanwhile, my dog waits at the back door because when she smells pancakes cooking, she knows that she will get at least two.)

The interesting thing about this "third idea back" is that, knowing the third idea is back there somewhere, you'd think that you could just ignore the first two ideas and act on the third. But it doesn't work that way. Idea Numbers One and Two just sit there stubbornly clogging up Idea Number Three. Until you have completely purged yourself of Ideas Number One and Two, magical Idea Number Three will not be born. In other words, you have to feed the first two pancakes to the dog in order to achieve a perfect pancake on your third try. The perfect idea can only come to light after two miserable ones.

Since this chapter is supposed to be about quilting and not pancakes, you can see where this is leading. Have you ever thrown out your first two fabric choices? Your first two blocks? Maybe you should. Sometimes we get stuck on our first idea and don't make way for the third. I have made entire quilts that look like Number One pancakes just because I was reluctant to change an initial idea. Ideas Number Two and Three just got tired of standing around waiting and eventually went home.

I don't know why the brain feels like it has to work this way. Why does it send out two decoy ideas before it will let out the third? And why doesn't the brain have some sort of numbering system for ideas so that you don't mistake Bad Idea Number Two for Good Idea Number Three? This is especially frustrating to me, as I am a sucker for Bad Idea Number Two which usually lurks in the shadows of my sewing room screaming, "Add some orange!" halfway through my quilt top.

Idea Number Two is a very pushy creature and must be firmly dealt with. Whenever the word "orange" pops into my head, I must delve into the cobwebby recesses of my brain and demand, "Is this Good Idea Number Three speaking . . . or Bad Idea Number Two?" At which point my husband usually walks into the room and offers me some sort of medication.

To further confuse you with my crude understanding of brain function, I also understand that all the really good creative ideas are born on the right side of the brain. The left side of your brain is where all the practical stuff is kept, like grocery lists and laundry stain removal charts. When you are quilting, the left side of your brain tells you when you have to stop, get up, and cook dinner. Obviously, the left side is sadly mistaken. You mustn't listen to it. Tune into the right side. The right side says things like, "Clean the house? Are you kidding?" and "Just quilt a little bit longer. Your family loves frozen entrees in little aluminum trays," and, my personal favorite, "Go on, buy that fabric. You deserve it." Just remember, the right side is always right.

I know your next question will be, "But Lisa, how do I know if my quilt idea is a left-brain idea or a right-brain idea? And how do I recognize if my idea is really the third one back?" And my answer will be a definite, "Don't ask me. I have no idea." To make matters worse, I just read that a team of medical experts has discovered that your right nostril smells things differently than your left nostril! With all these warring brain parts, it's amazing that we ever get any quilts made at all.

My advice is that you should just forget you ever read this chapter. I'm sure you have made perfectly lovely quilts in the past without having to know anything about brain anatomy, pancakes, nostrils, or anything of the sort. Do what you always have done, and simply listen to what your inner voice tells you. Just be sure to consult someone if you find you have more than one inner voice, especially if your inner voices start arguing. You might need a seriously long vacation —and just think of all the quilts you could make then!

Just One of the Sewing Machine Repair Dudes

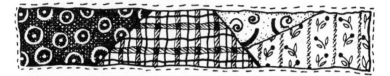

You might not be able to tell from where you're sitting, but I belong to an elite group of persons that share the celebrated title, "Sewing Machine Repair Dude." This title was not honorary; rather, it was earned by the skin of my knuckles and the ridicule of my peers. My climb to glory is one that was hard earned, as I started out in life as a mere non-mechanical, doll-playing, cake-baking female. My story is not a pretty one, but since you apparently have nothing else to do, I will relay it to you now.

My mother gave me my first sewing machine. It was a piece of garbage, but unfortunately, we didn't know it at the time. You'll remember that she won the beast in a scratch-off postcard promotion, and I naively assumed that all sewing machines were the same. I didn't notice that it didn't have a name brand on it, nor did I notice that all the motor specifications were written in the language of a primitive, hunter-gatherer tribe recently discovered in the innermost mountainous regions of a still-unnamed island.

The machine didn't even come with instructions, so when I needed to figure out simple situations like, "How do I keep the sewing machine from leaping off the table when I depress the pedal," I just had to solve the problem myself. With bricks, I decided.

I got to know that machine intimately, since its guts were usually strewn out all over my kitchen table. I learned how to repair sewing machines because I had no money to fix mine. It wasn't until years later, when I finally had to bring the beast to a repair shop to obtain a part, that I began to get the idea that my sewing machine was less than a quality instrument. After he stopped laughing at it, the sewing machine repair dude broke the news to me that there was no earthly way he could get parts for it. Sadly, I left the machine with him since he seemed so genuinely amused by it, gathered up my bricks, and went home.

I bought my next sewing machine 10 years later and couldn't believe how wonderful it was. It was only a simple mechanical zigzag machine, but it was a miracle to me. Why, I didn't even have to use my left hand anymore to keep the bobbin from falling out of the machine while I sewed! But my years of struggling with that other machine were not wasted, because I had gained intimate knowledge of the insides of a sewing machine. If I could repair the beast repeatedly, I could repair anything.

Unfortunately, since I was self-taught, I didn't quite know all the correct names for any of the dozens of complicated mechanisms inside. This posed a problem only after I began collecting various garage-sale sewing machines as a hobby. Some of these machines ended up needing parts, which I did not have and could not order by myself. And I knew, from previous experience with broken cars, that some repair men can try and pull one over on a novice, throwing around phrases like "kanuter valve" and words that end in "–adiator."

So when it came time to go to the local Sew 'n Vac, I had to steel myself and prepare mentally. I wanted to go down there and be able to ask confidently for a part, without giving away the fact that I was a mere self-taught, nail-filing, sweater-knitting female type. I need-ed to look like a real Sewing Machine Repair Dude.

I found a local sewing machine repair shop and swaggered in, my thumbs tucked in my belt loops, a well-placed smudge of sewing machine oil on my T-shirt. My attention was diverted immediately though, as the shop turned out to be a wondrous graveyard of old sewing machines and vacuums to die for! There was a Chinese hand-crankable sewing machine, replete with splendid gold decals of flying trapeze artists on it. There were beautiful old treadles and venerable old beauties of every make.

That Dorky Homemade Look

And I am not crazy about vacuum cleaners, but he had one there from 1935! After wiping the drool off my chin, I regained my composure and approached the repair dude behind the desk. Doing my best John Wayne, I slammed my broken part down on the counter in front of him. Making direct eye contact, I snapped my gum, narrowed my eyes, curled my thumbs back into my belt loops and sneered, "I need one of these here . . . um . . . bobbin . . . uh . . . bobbin . . . bobbin-adiators. Just give me what I want. I don't have all day."

Of course, my macho technique was less than perfect, but I needn't have worried. That day, I was lucky enough to make the acquaintance of a Number One Supreme Sewing Machine Dude. His love of old machines surpassed even my own, and he ended up giving me a tour of all the great stuff in his shop. In time, I had the opportunity to attend sewing machine repair classes and eventually learn the names of all the various anatomical parts.

I thought I was pretty sharp back in the days of the beast, but I soon learned that you need grease under the fingernails, pinched and skewered fingers, a few electrical shocks, and the consummate love of old machines to make you into a real Sewing Machine Repair Dude.

Wallflower Quilts

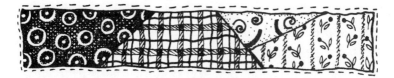

After 12 years of quilting and hundreds of quilt shows and classes to my credit, you'd think that I would get used to walking into a quilt show and seeing one of my own quilts on display. But the truth is that it always shocks me. I'll be walking along, oohing and aahhing over all the beautiful quilts on display; then I'll come to one that looks vaguely familiar. And just for an instant, before the recognition hits that it's one I've made, I get a feeling that this is a quilt that doesn't belong here. Finally, after years of wondering why, I think I know the reason.

At first I wondered if it was just insecurity. To me, quilts are so . . . well, personal. Seeing your own quilt on display is something like seeing yourself on video-tape for the first time. Isn't it shocking to see what you really look and sound like? I can't imagine being a movie star and having to watch a 12-foot tall picture of my face moving. I especially think my lips move real funny when I say words like "green beans" and "oranges." (If I ever get my big Hollywood break, I must have my agent specify that I won't do scenes about fruits and vegetables—I couldn't stand it.)

Seeing one of my quilts hanging on a public wall makes me feel like a little piece of my soul is on display for everyone to see. After all, a quilt involves hundreds of personal decisions. Everything from fabric color to type of binding is carefully considered. Each fabric has a little history. You bought that purple, viney floral the day you went shopping with your friends and got so silly at lunchtime, remember? And each stitch is a moment frozen in time. Recall how you were making this block when the phone rang announcing your new grandchild? A quilt is a time capsule of events, a reflection of tastes, thoughts, moods, and feelings. And there it waves, out in the open, for everyone to examine and wonder about you. Frankly, I have far too many people wondering about me as it is.

Today I saw a quilt of mine at a quilt show and decided that it wasn't just insecurity that made me cringe when I saw it. As a matter of fact, I had an epiphany of sorts, so I decided to rush home and write about it. I hope you appreciate the research I did, as it required several trips around the quilt show, pretending to be surprised whenever I came upon my own quilt. Over and over, I would round the corner, hum te dum, and then, "Why lookee here, what is this one about?"

After I did this a few times, I realized what made mine different! Mine didn't belong with the others because my quilts don't belong on display! My quilts belong crumpled up in little heaps on beds piled high with pillows. My quilts belong thrown over shivery cold legs on winter nights. My quilts belong trailing behind drooling toddlers and wrapped around crying teenagers. It's no wonder that my quilt looked funny hanging there on display, all spread-eagled and flat and lonely with a sign that commanded "DO NOT TOUCH!" on it. Suddenly, I felt like I had placed my beloved pet in a zoo.

Now don't get mad at me. I love art quilts. I love quilts with a theme and careful color balance and a planned message. I love precise, traditional applique and marvel at the skill of the quiltmaker. I love that some of us have taken quilts to the level of fine art. I'm just saying that the joy of quiltmaking for me is not purely in the visual impact, but it's textural and con-textual also. In other words, the quilts I make are not just to be looked at. My quilts are soft and fluffy and cuddly. My quilts actively participate in my life and comfort those that I love. They are beautiful to me because they call out to be touched and held. To look at them is to understand only a small part of their characters.

If I ever had my own quilt show, I would have all visitors sit in big comfy easy chairs and tuck quilts around themselves. Some soft music would be lovely, and maybe a nice tray of cookies and hot tea. "Relax," I would say, "don't worry about a thing."

Yes, I know that this is highly impractical. At the end of my show, I would have dozens of people snoring away in the armchairs, spilling tea, and getting cookie crumbs all over my works of art. (I know this for a fact because it happens most every night at nine o'clock in my living room.)

I suppose that it was a big step in the evolution of quilts that they finally did escape the living room and cookie crumbs and made their way into museums as fine art. I thank my quilting sisters for that huge accomplishment.

It is yet another wonder of quiltmaking that we all belong in it, no matter the type of quilts we make. Some quilts remind us of where we are going; some remind us of where we have been.

So I hope I have given you something to think about. In short, the next time you go to a quilt show, take time to notice the quilts that you could easily walk right past without a second glance. Like a plain and lovely woman, each has a quiet message all its own.

Porky Pig's Place

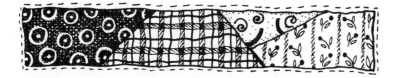

When I was in my late teens and early 20s, I loved fashion magazines. I read with rapt attention every time a new hairspray was invented, pored over ads searching for new colors of lipstick, and dutifully studied the step-by-step photographs of how to create the Farrah Fawcett hairdo. This was important stuff to me. I remember one particular article distinctly as it dealt with the annoying problem of how to sit on your towel at the beach. As I recall (take notes if you missed this), you should NEVER, I repeat NEVER, just flop out your beach towel and sit upon it. Why, that is practically disgusting. You need to pre-roll your towel at home, then flip it gracefully in the air and onto the sand.

Next, when crossing your ankles, slide your back leg forward and sink gracefully down onto your towel. For heaven's sake, don't ever let your thighs touch the towel. You must keep your knees elevated so that your thighs hang down instead of being flattened against the towel. If you perform this sitting position properly, the size of your thighs is minimized. People at the beach will marvel at your lack of thighs. They will all stare at you, wondering where your thighs went. Lifeguards will ask you for your phone number. At least, that's the way I remember it.

Funny how ridiculous that all seemed when I became a 30-something married homeowner. All the attention I used to lavish so carefully upon my cuticles became focused upon my house. I subscribed to all the Home and Garden magazines and worried about tile colors and floral arrangements and if striped pillowcases could be successfully paired with floral sheets. My towels matched their respective bathrooms and my home was a showplace. That is, until my son was born and embarked on his current 12-year mission to seek and destroy . . . well, *everything*. Should he choose to pursue it, I believe he has a fine future ahead of him as an interior desecrator.

Now that I am 40, I wonder why I used to worry so much about my looks and my house. My looks are fine—or maybe I am just finally used to me now. I sure don't care about my thighs at the beach (the lifeguard is still mildly interesting, although I don't think it's very wise to entrust mere toddlers to that position, do you?). My house, well, I can't say that I even know what happened there. But I do have a theory. I think my tastes are regressing to when I was around five years old.

You see, when I was five, I loved cartoons. More specifically, I loved watching Bugs Bunny and Porky Pig. Not because of their antics, but because of the soft, pretty little world they lived in. I especially loved Porky's house. The armchairs were huge and over-stuffed, and all of the furniture was rounded and generous and had little doilies sitting on top. His tables were lovingly covered with softly flowing cloth, and billowy curtains were gently tied back at every window.

Porky cared nothing for antiques or pretentious decoration. His art was limited to gently rolling landscapes, and everything in his house was the color of jelly beans. Porky was gloriously pink and round and proud of it. Porky was comfortable in his house and comfortable with himself. Porky was my idol.

Now that I am 40-something, I think I'm in a Porky flashback phase. I try to re-create the peace and gentility of my favorite pig idol in my everyday life. My furnishings are overstuffed and my shoes are sensible. My quilts tend to be soft and flowing and the color of Easter morning. More importantly, I long to feel as comfortable in my skin as Porky did in his.

Recounting my life like this, I have to wonder what my 50s have in store for me. I wonder what kind of quilts I'll be making then. I wonder if I will be craving excitement and making quilts with lots of red and orange. Will I be doing contemporary quilts? Will I like pointy patterns with sharp angles? Will I look back at my current Porky era as a frumpy, self-satisfied time in my life?

I think the exciting thing about looking ahead is the knowledge that quilting will be a part of my life until the day that I leave this earth. I look forward to the phases I will go through and know that quilting will provide me a solace and comfort even when I take my veiny, flabby thighs to the beach and shamelessly plop them down flat on my beach towel.

I will always have a quilt in my head to make and, therefore, a reason to get up in the morning. As a matter of fact, are any of you free to go fabric shopping with me on my hundredth birthday? I'll pick you up on my motorcycle. I just hope you don't mind sharing a seat with the lifeguard . . . .

The Beast

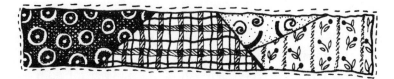

I used to try and get my husband involved in quilting. I thought for sure that once I dragged him to his first quilt show, he would fall under the same spell that has bewitched me for 14 years. I had visions of bringing him to fabric shops and having him help me pick out fabrics. Then, of course, I hoped that he would become interested in all the quilting tools and gadgets that I love so much! I wished that the new and improved sewing machines equipped with the latest features would dance through his dreams at night, just like they do in mine.

But after several years of finding him back at the car reading a book whenever I dragged him on a quilting excursion, I had just about given up hope. So it was a surprise to me when he became interested in my latest quilting quest: I wanted a long-arm quilting machine.

The first time I showed him a picture of the long-arm industrial machine, his eyes lit up. At the time, I was excited that he was finally showing interest.

That Dorky Homemade Look

Unfortunately, I should have realized that showing my husband anything with a big motor on it was a mistake. The die was cast; my fate was sealed. I was about to meet . . . THE BEAST.

The Beast came into my life without warning on a fine Saturday morning in April. I was leaving for a quilting class (and I was running a tad late, as usual), when my husband came riding up the driveway on his bicycle with a flushed grin on his face. That familiar "uh-oh" feeling came over me. I knew he had been out cruising garage sales, and the last time he came back with that look, something very large and rusty came to live with us and never went away. "Honey!" he exclaimed as I winced, bracing myself for the worst, "I bought you a long-arm machine!"

My reaction was one of momentary elation, followed by a "Hey, wait a minute . . . this is my husband . . . oh no . . . what did he buy now?" But before panic set in, I thought I better look at the thing. It couldn't be as bad as the 13 rusty juicers or the 1940 Packard he had brought home previously. So, with fear in my heart, I followed him out to the neighborhood garage sale to help him load the machine into our family truck.

I got my first glimpse of the machine through a voluminous curtain of old clothes, which hung from the garage ceiling all around us. My husband led me through the packed clothing, carefully parting the way like a jungle safari guide. That's when I saw THE

BEAST. It was huge. It was old and ugly and monstrous. It was a horrible shade of gray and it was covered with dirt, rust, spiderwebs, and pet hair. I yelped and leapt back, hoping it didn't bite. Trying to remain positive (and calm), I turned to my husband. "This?" was the only thing I could manage to say.

Meanwhile, my husband was busying himself, trying to figure out how to move it. He picked up one edge of it and made a sound like "woof," so I knew it wasn't going to be easy. Meanwhile, the garage-sale lady, who spoke little English, ran in circles around the machine shaking her head and shouting, "Heaby! Eees berrry heaby!"

She was right; it was berry heaby. Somehow we managed to get it home after breaking only one spool pin, scraping the truck paint, and spilling a whole gallon of lubricating oil all over the truck bed. While I was at quilt class, my husband and son brought the Beast into our foyer, which was as far as they could move it because my husband injured his back unloading it.

When I got home that night, the Beast was in the foyer to greet me, drooling oil, wheezing, and smelling like a wet dog. I finally figured out what attracted my husband to it. It had a motor on it that could double as a booster rocket on a space station. When he pushed the "On" button, the floor rumbled as the Beast powered up, ready to quilt that iron and steel quilt I had been planning all along. My husband stood there, hunched over with back pain, absolutely radiant with happiness. "What a machine!" he said proudly.

Ah, but if that were only the end of this sad tale. You'd think that having to live with a gray, rusty, oozing industrial machine the size of Vermont in your foyer would be enough. Unfortunately, my husband then dropped the final bomb: "Happy Anniversary," he said lovingly, smiling past his back pain, as I realized that I was looking at my seventeenth wedding anniversary gift. Wow, talk about a gift that just keeps on giving . . .

I think the moral to this sad tale is this: I now think that it is okay to have separate interests from one's spouse. I will now encourage his rusty sprinkler collection and smile when he brings home another box of old telephone parts. I now understand that he is just as mystified at my interest in quilting as I am with his fascination for anything rusty. He is the light and love of my life, and I don't care whether he ever attends a quilt show with me or not. Hmmmm, I wonder if that was his plan all along . . . .

What's Your PQ?

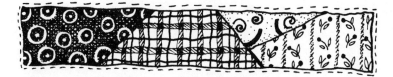

Whenever I teach a new group of students, I try to find out as much as I can about them in advance. I often ask each of them to bring in a piece of their work and describe what kind of quilting they like best. Sometimes I ask careful questions about their attitude toward seam-ripping. As they tell me about themselves, I must confess that I am secretly sizing them up. My hidden mission? Before I teach them anything, I'm carefully calculating their PQ.

What is a PQ? A PQ, or "Perfection Quotient," is a highly sophisticated mathematical expression that I invented. When I carefully calculate your PQ using my advanced knowledge of trigonometry and calculus, your PQ will tell me how much of a quilting perfectionist you are. Well, truthfully, I haven't quite figured out the equation yet, but it will have something to do with the number of mangled triangles in your quilt divided by the total number of pointy ones. I'll have to multiply something by how many minutes you are willing to spend with a seam ripper and subtract something if I ever hear you say anything like, "Oh well, no one will notice."

Unfortunately, I have more time for quilting than I have for math, so I'm still working on the math part of the equation. In the meantime, I rate students on a subjective scale from one to ten, a "One" being an extremely carefree quilter and "Ten" being a hopeless fussbudget.

I rate myself as an "Eight" on the PQ scale. (I have to say "Eight" because I'm writing a chapter that my students will read. I'm probably more like a "Seven," but don't let that get around.) I strive for perfection, but I'll only rip out a seam a maximum of three times before I give up on it. I used to be a "Nine," but I got over that since turning 40. Come to think of it, that's when I gave up on an immaculate house and the perfect pie crust, too—must have been a virus or something.

Once you've discovered your own PQ, you may find that it will fluctuate. I've found that my personal PQ can fluctuate according to what I call the "Aunt Irma or Uncle Fred" factor. Am I making this quilt for Aunt Irma, the woman who irons her bed sheets? If so, I try to sew like a "Nine." On the other hand, if the quilt is for Uncle Fred (who has no idea what a bed sheet is for), then I can relax and sew like a "Five."

I love to teach a classroom full of students with PQ's of "One" through "Six." They're so easy to please and they believe everything I say! "Ones" through "Sixes" would be the first to admit that they would rather eat a bug than to use their seam rippers. Unfortunately, they also think that I am a hopeless fussbudget, as I'm always pointing out tiresome things like "Hmmm, this fabric was supposed to have been sewn on right side up" and "Oops, that quarter-inch seam allowance looks a mite hefty. You might want to narrow it down an inch or two."

"Sevens," "Eights," and "Nines" are more of a challenge to teach, but they are careful listeners and make beautiful quilts. "Sevens" through "Nines" make frequent use of their seam rippers. They often ask me, "Should I rip this out?" which is really a very funny question, if you think about it. What they're really hoping to hear is, "No, don't bother." But just for the fun of it, sometimes I look each of them meaningfully in the eye, gaze deep into each one's soul and ask, "Does this mistake bother *you*? Are you going to be able to live with this mistake for the rest of your life? Will this mistake be the last thing you think about as you take your final breath? If the answer is yes, then by all means, rip it out." Students look pretty dazed as they head back to their seats, but, hopefully, I've given them something to ponder.

As a teacher, I live in fear of getting a student with a PQ of "Ten" in one of my classes. "Tens" deserve a "Ten" as a teacher. I'm afraid that the "Tens" in my class will be terribly disappointed when they find out that I'm a mere "Seven" masquerading as an "Eight"!

When I have a "Ten" student in my classroom, the challenge is not to let on that, when compared to her high standards, I'm a total slob. I try to give her "Ten" answers when she askes me questions like, "Should I take out this half-stitch?" and "Do you think anyone will notice that I cut off a bit of this bee antenna?"

Yes, yes, the answer is always yes. "Take out everything. Sew backwards, as a matter of fact. Iron that again. Yes, it will haunt you for the rest of your life that this miniscule flower in your floral print is upside down. Take it out and try again."

Teaching a "Ten" can be an exhausting experience, but the quilt world is lucky to have them. "Tens" make the quilts that make history—quilts so awesome in their workmanship that they inspire every one of us to raise our own PQ's.

So what is your PQ? Are you a happy-go-lucky "One" or a masterful "Ten"? Whatever your number, the important thing is to maintain your joy in quilting. Don't stress out for Aunt Irma and don't cop out for Uncle Fred. Wear your own number proudly, and, for goodness sake, stop ironing your sheets. Life is short. Go make a quilt instead.

Yes, But What Else Do You Do?

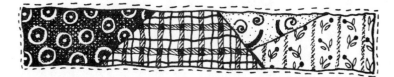

When I lecture or teach a class, at the end of each session I usually ask if anyone has any questions. Inevitably, without fail, the first question will be, "How long does it take you to make a quilt?" After that question, I am ready for the next question, which is always, without fail, "What kind of batting do you use?" I should take the time to answer these questions right now so that anyone who reads this chapter will never have to ask again. In order, the answers to these questions are: it depends and it depends. There, now that that's settled, it's my turn, and I am dying to ask each of *you* a question. Now please don't answer all at once, because I really would like to hear each and every answer.

My question to you is: what else do you do while you are quilting? I have a hard time with this question. I have no problem picking out batting (I told you . . . it depends), but I have a real problem trying to entertain myself. I've found that I must do something else, because when I am sitting at my sewing machine just chain-sewing triangles together, I have to keep my mind busy. With a mind like mine, I just can't let it go wandering off any time it feels like it. Sometimes it doesn't come back when I call it.

I know a lot of people who watch television while they are quilting. Television doesn't quite work for me. When I turn on the TV, I get interested in the TV program instead of sewing my triangles. An hour will pass by, and there I sit, still staring at the TV with only one triangle completed.

One friend suggested trying to watch something boring, but that doesn't work either, because no matter how boring it is, it's still more interesting than chain piecing 866 triangles together. Other friends watch talk shows, but frankly, those shows are just too weird. Their guests must be from another planet because they have waaaaay different problems than mine. They can't decide who fathered their children or just when their boyfriends started running around with their mothers. My only crisis during the day is to decide what kind of green vegetable to have with supper. Why can't they have a talk show entitled, "I Served Peas When My Husband Wanted Brussels Sprouts"?

Talking on the phone is not good either. I can't talk and sew at the same time. I really don't know why this is, but I do have a theory. Just like my stash has taken over the spare room, I think quilting thoughts have overtaken the talking center in my brain. Now guests can't use the spare room and I can't talk when I'm sewing. (I think it makes perfect sense. Fortunately my brain logic centers are still intact.) Listening to talking seems to be kay; I like it when my mother calls because she can talk for several hours straight without requiring any input on my part. Even an occasional "uh-huh" from my side throws her rhythm off. If you want her number, just let me know. I don't think she'd mind you calling; you can pretend that you're me. She hasn't heard me say anything but "uh-huh" for so long that I don't think she would be able to tell the difference.

After several years of experimenting, I've found the best solution to be music. Listening to music helps me stay in the present, but it's not exciting enough to be distracting. I do have to be careful not to listen to anything with a beat, though, as a beat can make me start dancing around my sewing room. This not only looks unseemly, but I've found that doing "The Macarena" can be downright dangerous when I am holding a rotary cutter.

Classical music is almost perfect. I love Chopin and Rachmaninoff, but unfortunately, and I don't know if you've heard, but they're dead. The problem with dead composers is that they have a tendency to write unfinished symphonies, which is very depressing and can lead to unfinished quilts. Being dead, they also tend to

write very little new music, which means I have to listen to the same classical music over and over again and
. . . oooops! My mind starts wandering again, and,
before you know it, I come up with ideas for articles
like this one, and then you have to read all about it.

In conclusion, if you have successfully solved this
problem, consider yourself lucky. By the way, what
kind of batting do you use?

The Fabric Funny Farm

You never know when one of those "Aha!" moments is going to strike. You know, those moments in quilting when that little cartoon light bulb hovering over your head suddenly brightens to a blaring, blinding, thousand-watt headlamp. All of a sudden, things fall into place. Niggling questions you have bounced around for years finally jump from the UFO bin in your brain to the "ready-for-binding" area of your mind. Sometimes these magical moments float gently from above and land softly upon your head. But other times, an awareness comes out of nowhere and blindsides you like a freight train.

I had one of these freight-train moments yesterday. I was watching a quilting show on TV, and the guest quilter was talking about how she arranges her stash. I, of course, like many other quilters, have always arranged my stash according to color. A pile of red here, a pile of green there, and so on; nothing very exciting. So my ears perked up when this guest quilter began talking about a different classification system. It seems that this particular quilter sorts her fabrics, she said . . . get this . . . by MOOD.

"Holey moley!" I thought to myself, "fabrics have moods?" All of a sudden, the quilting universe fell into perfect order. Fabrics have moods. Well, well. That just about explains everything for me. Today, armed with this new knowledge, I have been busy closely examining and re-organizing my fabric stash, psychoanalyzing each piece. "Tell me about yourself," I think, as I try to tune into my fabric's disposition. "How are you feeling today?"

My biggest surprise was how many of my fabrics turned up in the cranky pile. I had no idea that I had been buying such ill-natured yardage. This explains a lot of my quilting problems. My cranky stuff is fully of pointy, spiky little things that are control freaks. They don't want to work with any other fabrics and are always bickering when I try to put them in a block together.

My best quilt plans are often ruined by these little monsters. How can I sew anything with my fabric in such a bad mood? You can bet I'm vowing to stop making this mistake when I visit the quilt shop. I'm going to grasp each fabric firmly by its bolt and demand to know, "Are you a nice fabric or a crabby fabric? Are you gonna work with me, or am I gonna have to get rough with you?" (Oh, don't worry, my fabric shop has gotten used to me.)

I suppose it's partially my fault. I'm always attracted to the brooding loners on the sale shelf. It's just that they look like they need a friend, you know? Some of them can be irritable, yes, but many of them just suffer from depression. You would be depressed, too, if you were a droopy gray floral or a geometric that looks like it's got bugs crawling on it.

Unfortunately, I have taken home more than my fair share of really depressed fabrics. Even more unfortunately, I have never found an effective way of cheering them up. They just seem to depress all the other fabrics. Why, I witnessed one particularly morose burgundy solid make a Debbie Mumm fabric cry! My heart is in the right place, but I realize now that these moody fabrics need to be treated by a professional quilt artist whose skills at fabric psychology are greater than mine. Harriet, Judy, Carol? If you're reading this (and I'm sure you are!), come and pick up this fabric. It's beyond my help.

The news is not all bad though. For fabrics with mild personality disorders, a group-therapy program may be effective. For example, I had some fabrics from the '70s that seemed to be going through some sort of mid-life crisis. They just couldn't accept the fact that calico was dead and that they needed to get on with their lives. So I decided to move my '70s fabrics right next to my hopelessly cheery '30s reproduction prints. My '30s prints are absolutely giddy with happiness, but definitely in denial. (Are they naïve or what? There was a depression going on, for goodness sakes!) Together, the '30s fabrics and the '70s fabrics balanced each other out and now lead happy shelf-lives. My '60s fabrics will be okay one day, too, as soon as the flashbacks stop.

I suppose that it's a good thing, paying attention to the many moods of my fabric. But sometimes I step into my sewing room, face all my stacks of moody fabrics and ask them, "Hey! What about *my* needs?" This has led me to the conclusion that fabric must be male, because all I get in response is a blank stare. Uh-oh, another light-bulb moment.

Make Your Husband Read This

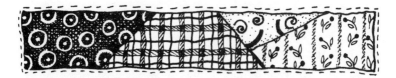

Honestly, my husband is pitiful when it comes to picking out presents. He tries really hard, and sometimes spends lots of money, but the problem is not the effort or the money. The real problem is that he just doesn't *care*. Oh, I'm not saying he doesn't care about me! We have been married for 16 wonderful years. He is the most loving, kind-hearted man in the world. And he loves me like crazy, too. What he doesn't care about are the presents themselves. He doesn't like presents. He doesn't like getting them, and he sure doesn't like having to pick them out for someone else.

I don't know exactly how he got this way. I think that part of it is just being a man. I believe when men are boys, they get really excited about presents. Chemistry sets, pocketknives, collections of dead bugs with pins through them—what's not to get excited about? But alas, after a certain age, every man inevitably enters the dreaded Tie and Cologne Phase of Life. Poor, poor men. No wonder they get depressed around Christmas-time. It would be hard to try and muster any enthusiasm opening up your third "Flashlight with Portable Radio" or seventh "Wonder Tool that Does Everything."

I noticed one year, when I was a young bride, that I kept buying my husband stuff to save us in an emergency. For years, I gave him emergency road kits (complete with flares and snakebite anti-venom!), first-aid kits, and survival gear . . . yikes! What a responsibility I was handing him! And what was infinitely worse in his mind was that if we were ever in a flash flood, I could yell, "What!?! Where is that emergency life raft I gave you for Valentine's Day?"

So it should come as no surprise that gifts are not an exciting thing for most men. It really is too bad, because all the women I know still feel the same way about presents as they did when Santa Claus brought them down the chimney. I love presents. And I think I can safely say, with few exceptions, that quilters love presents. After all, there is so much to love.

Even if you do have all the tools you could ever use (hmmm . . . impossible), there's all that fabric! Every time you think you have seen it all, here comes the delivery truck to your local fabric shop, and poof. Out come the new bolts of luscious fabric, and you simply must have more. But you rarely see men standing around delivery trucks at the local hardware store, anxiously waiting for new boxes of hammers to be opened.

This is because hardware is boring and it smells funny. No wonder men don't understand the gift thing.

One of the most romantic things my husband ever did for me was in 1984. I remember the year exactly because at the time, he was only a boyfriend. But this one deed scooped him out of the murky depths of the boyfriend bin and plopped him neatly into the marriage material receptacle. What was this wonderful deed? I'll tell you, but you have to promise not to swoon.

At the time, in 1984, I hadn't yet discovered quilting. I had discovered cross-stitch, though, and spent quite a bit of my leisure time hunched over, counting teeny-tiny holes in aida cloth. I was working on a large sampler and whining every time I had to face traffic to go buy a new color of embroidery floss. So one day when I was at work, my wonderful manly man carted my entire embroidery thread collection to the local stitchery store, and he bought every single color of floss that I didn't already own! Can you imagine how wonderful it was, as a cross-stitcher, to open up a big, beautifully-wrapped box stuffed with hundreds of colors of thread? Oh, it makes my heart go pitty-pat to think of it. What a man.

Unfortunately, what makes this so memorable is that it was the last time he did it. I keep hoping that, now that I'm a quilter, he'll get the same idea with the Bali fabric collection. "Oh my stars, honey, I just wish I had every single one of these colors!" I say in my best

Scarlett O'Hara voice. But somehow my eyelashes don't get me as far as they used to. For one of my birthdays (and I am really not making this up!), I got a carrot peeler. Now, it was a really great carrot peeler and I still have it, but really! A carrot peeler! Can you imagine?

Now I'm not saying the carrot peeler was a bad present. I have gotten so much mileage out of this carrot peeler story that I wouldn't trade it for a diamond ring! My husband, bless his heart, has had to hear me tell the carrot-peeler-birthday-present-story to my friends and public for several years now. I even won a free dinner on a radio show by telling it over the airwaves to thousands of people! Poor guy, I have to shame him into buying me better presents by waving around my carrot peeler. It's a wonder he hasn't stolen it away and buried it in the backyard by now.

Wouldn't you just go weak in the knees if your significant other handed you a heavy box and said something like, "Sweetheart, I noticed that your fabric stash was somewhat lacking in the tone-on-tone primary colors, so I went out and bought you a collection." Or, "Honey, I was just passing by your favorite quilt shop and noticed these new Alexander Henry prints in several colorways—I do hope you like them." Honestly, at that point, Fabio couldn't look any better, could he? Forget what they say about men and babies—wouldn't you just drool over a man with fabric?

Okay, I know, it's pretty impossible. But just for fun, why don't you leave this article lying out on the countertop somewhere. You know, just toss it casually upon the countertop, maybe with some subtle red arrows and maybe his name at the top? Hmmm, knowing the male psyche, you'd better laminate this article and epoxy it to his carburetor. Or maybe to his forehead. In any event, let him know that he can walk into a quilt shop at any time, maybe even on the way home from work, and pick you up a little fat quarter or two. Now that's romantic!

The Quilting Quagmire

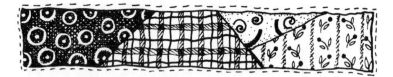

I've sure gotten a lot of cleaning done lately. I've cleared out drawers, alphabetized my spices, and even vacuumed behind the refrigerator. Come to think of it, I've gotten a lot of cooking and laundry done lately, too. Too bad I haven't done any quilting. I haven't even been in my sewing room for days. You see, there's a problem in there. It's a big problem, too. The floor of my sewing room has disappeared and, in its place, a giant mucky swamp full of quicksand-like goop has appeared.

I'm actually very lucky in here, hiding out in the . . . ugh . . . kitchen . . . because the mucky ooze in my sewing room has it in for me. Right now, I can hear it making sucking, slurping noises as it devours all the remaining creativity and ambition right out of the atmosphere. Oh well, maybe I can find some knick-knacks to dust or something.

Okay, okay, so I'm being dramatic. There isn't really any goo in my sewing room; it just feels that way. I'm avoiding my sewing room because there's a decision to be made in there, and I can't seem to make it. I'm stuck creatively, just as if I were mired in quicksand. This happens to me occasionally. I get "decision-phobic."

I'll stand there, sometimes for hours, contemplating a pieced versus a plain border. I'll go back and forth, then decide on a multiple border. After I struggle with that concept for a while, I get the feeling that maybe no border at all would be best. Uh-oh . . . can you feel it? Here comes the creative quicksand, starting to ooze up from the floor, seeping through my toes, preparing to bog me down with eternal indecision.

If any of this sounds familiar to you, you're not alone. The Quilting Quagmire, as I have named this phenomenon, happens to everyone. Sometimes it can come upon you suddenly over a very simple thing, such as whether or not to re-sew a seam or just leave it be. But the stickiest, gummiest, gorpiest quagmires involve really complicated issues.

Oh, it starts out simply enough, such as "What kind of fabric should I use for this little snowman's nose?" But then, like primordial slime, the question grows ominously. For you see, if you decide to use that shade of orange, it doesn't go with the orange in the border fabric, does it? And if you can't use that border fabric, what border fabric will you use? Hmmm, you could use the fabric you were planning to use for your nephew's quilt, but then, you wouldn't have enough left over for the binding for your daughter's quilt. Maybe if you changed the floral fabric in your maple leaf quilt, you would have enough orange, or maybe if you changed the background of the leaf, you could use that blue instead. But, then you would have to change the green that went with the blue . . . .you see what I'm getting at? An entire cascade of decisions you don't want to make, all because of a snowman's nose! Arrrggggh!

As you run like a screaming crazy woman out of your sewing room, you can hear the quagmire making victorious sucking and gurgling noises behind you. Phew! You got out this time . . . go cook something and forget about it.

Fortunately there's a way to defeat the quilting quagmire, but it's not easy, and sometimes it can get downright ugly. I know from experience, because I used to be constantly stuck in the muck. So please, take my valuable advice, as it comes from years of painful cooking and cleaning experiences—anything to avoid the decisions in the sewing room! Here's the key to defeating the quagmire: learn to love your decisions, no matter what. Make the best decision you can, execute it, and learn to love your results. You can even learn to love your mistakes, because how else are you really ever going to learn?

I have learned many rewarding lessons by just leaping forward and doing something, no matter what. If

I'm slightly less in love with the results than I should be, I think, "Oh well, I could make this quilt again except do that part differently—if I wanted to." This usually stops my whining, because if there's anything that I hate to do, it's making the same quilt twice. I'd rather eat fish heads than make the same quilt all over again. So with that as a threat, I decide I just *looooooove* the quilt exactly how it is and have no desire to do it any differently.

So there's my advice on vanquishing the Quilting Quagmire. And now that I've written an entire essay on it, I guess it's time for me to get up out of this chair and brave the muck in my own sewing room. My particular problem this time is that I want to do a scalloped border on a butterfly quilt, but I have no idea how wide to make it. Now that I've put my problem into words, it sounds like a pretty silly reason to avoid my sewing room. Whew, I've spent three days cleaning and cooking, when I could have just decided to make the border six inches wide and live with the result. Okay, six inches wide it is. Uh-oh, should I cut the binding on the bias, or . . . . . . oh no!

The
Tissue Issue

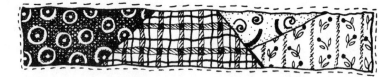

It has recently come to my attention that there is a national commercial gracing the airwaves that shows a group of sweet little cartoon women quilting. There they sit, waving their needles about, busily sewing, having a lovely chat just like at an old-fashioned quilting bee. Have you seen it? Oh yeah, I forgot to mention . . . they're quilting toilet paper! And they're absolutely gushing about the virtues of this particular brand being superior. It's softer and fluffier because it's **quilted**!

Have you ever quilted toilet paper? Me neither. I wonder why these wee cartoon ladies got the urge. Did they run out of fabric? Batting? Or was it a creative decision? Is it an ultra-kitschy, fiber-art thing? Are they making an artistic statement about quilt art in the post-modern age? I've decided that it must be a far deeper statement than it seems, i.e., just a group of modern women, sitting around quilting a roll of toilet paper. There must be a message in there somewhere, addressing the social and political concerns of the modern woman. One day I'll figure it out.

Come to think of it, I've never heard the topic discussed at any quilt guild meeting I've ever been to. Maybe it's an important topic that we should address: "To Quilt, or Not to Quilt, Your Toilet Paper?" Now I'll admit that once or twice in the past, I have bought toilet paper with little flowers or elves on it, but that's the farthest I've ever ventured into the realm of toilet-paper embellishment. I did know a woman once who would fold the first unused sheet of her toilet paper into a "V" shape to make it easier for her guests to find the next unused sheet (it must have been a terrible problem at her parties).

Maybe one day, our collective consciousness will be raised enough to put this long-neglected toilet-paper quilting issue on our guild agendas. Too many quilters ignore the question. I, myself, have deliberately gone to guild meetings in order to escape my toilet paper. And when I get there, I hardly even think about toilet paper . . . well, except if they're serving coffee and it's been a really long meeting. Meanwhile, there it sits at home, unembellished, un-quilted by loving hands, and without a little "V" folded into it. Oh dear, now I feel so guilty.

I wonder what enlightened advertising executive finally thought to bring this tissue issue to our attention. Here's the picture I get: a board room meeting full of men in dark blue suits sitting around a large oblong table. The advertising executive in charge of this particular toilet paper account stands and begins his pitch. "Here's my idea: there's this huge roll of cartoon toilet paper, see? Sitting around it are these teeny-weeny quilter women, gossiping about toilet paper like quilters often do. These petite, waif-like women are hard at work, lovingly hand-quilting this humongous roll of toilet paper, 12 to 14 stitches per inch. All the while they are so excited and happy, because after they are done quilting it, they know that it is very, very soft—quilted, as a matter of fact—and they just can't wait for you to apply their loving handiwork to . . . well, you know. Women will love it!"

I'd be willing to wager that this particular ad exec's wife is not a quilter. And if she isn't, I'm pretty sure that those cartoon artists had to call in quilting consultants. They would have had to ask a real quilter the question: "If you were going to quilt your toilet paper, how would you do it?" Personally, I would have suggested a quilting frame. Now, I'm not a stickler for realism, but those little women are not even using a hoop! And they didn't put a stitch of basting in that toilet paper, from what I could see.

Honestly, you would think that they would take some responsibility as far as accuracy for those of us who would like to try it at home. Come to think of it, maybe they don't want us to try it at home. What if the toilet paper quilting hobby really caught on? No one would buy their toilet paper. I'm sure that's the reason they didn't shoot for accuracy; they didn't want to give away company secrets. That must be it.

I think that one day I will finally grasp the complexity of this advertising promotion. I vow to someday understand the angst of my tiny little quilting sisters, who by choice or by force (who knows which?) are devoting their lives to unselfishly quilting my toilet paper. Thank you, little ladies. Thank you for doing that for me; thank you for the time you have saved me. I now have time for more important things, like hand-painting my Kleenex and monogramming my sponges. And thank you, too, television. Once again, you have given us something to think about.

About
the Author

Lisa Boyer made her first dorky homemade quilt top at the age of eight. Lisa holds a degree in Microbiology and Psychology, worked as a Clinical Laboratory scientist, then became a quilter, pattern-designer, sewing-machine mechanic, quilt teacher, writer, magazine columnist, and mother. Her varied interests have led her to write articles on such diverse topics as quilting, hurricanes, vegetables, shoes, and sewing-machine repair, just to name a few.

Lisa Boyer's quirky sense of humor has been delighting readers of *Quilting Today Magazine* for over three years. Known to her friends as "the mad scientist," Lisa combines her love of quilting with her background in physics and chemistry, resulting in some strangely unique philosophies.

Lisa Boyer is a native southern Californian, but has lived in northern California and Oregon, as well. She now lives on the Hawaiian island of Kauai with her husband and son.

Lisa's articles have appeared in *Kauai Magazine* and the *Orange County Register*, in addition to *Quilting Today Magazine*.

Lisa's quilts have appeared in *Quilting Today, Miniature Quilts,* and *Kauai* magazines.